Ladies
of Distinction
IN NORTHAMPTONSHIRE

*A pot-pourri of charismatic women
from all walks of life*

Mia Butler
and Colin Eaton

JOHN NICKALLS PUBLICATIONS

PREVIOUSLY PUBLISHED
BY MIA BUTLER

Northamptonshire Rambles 1991

Exploring the Nene Way 1992

Secrets and Treasures of Northamptonshire 1996

Let's Go Walkabout in Northamptonshire 1996

A Northamptonshire Quiz Book 1997

*Learn Yersalf Northamptonshire Dialect
(with Colin Eaton)* 1998

*Walks in Mysterious Northamptonshire
(with Marian Pipe)* 1999

*A Second Northamptonshire Quiz Book
(with Colin Eaton)* 2000

Nature Trails in Northamptonshire 2002

*Tipple & Teashop Rambles
in Northamptonshire* 2004

ISBN 1 904136 24 9

Published by John Nickalls Publications
Oak Farm Bungalow, Sawyers Lane, Suton,
Wymondham, Norfolk NR18 9SH

Designed by Ashley Gray and Printed by Barnwell's Print Limited,
Penfold Street, Aylsham, Norfolk NR11 6ET

CONTENTS

INTRODUCTION. V

Joan Hickson 1

Anne Bracegirdle. 5

Anne Bradstreet. 8

Bernice Field 17

Bertha Willmott. 26

Caroline Bradley 31

Caroline Chisholm. 36

Courtney Hope. 46

Elizabeth Jean Harwood 50

Elizabeth Woodville. 54

Mary L Pendered 56

Ruby Murray 59

Sister Mary Ward. 65

Aelfgifu of Northampton. 70

Lady Adeline of Deene Park 73

Annie Louisa Bagshaw 77

Dr Grace Thornton 82

Lady Ethel Wickham. 85

Dame Edith Sitwell 88

Kathleen Lilian 'Bill' Coggins 92

Lady Diana Spencer 95

Maria von Sandizell. 97

Miss Cecil Wilson MacQueen. 101

Princess Alice 104

CAMEOS

Alice Old 107

Boudicca 107

Celia Fiennes 109

Cherrynose 109

Lady Hatton 110

Ghosts galore 110

Hannah Sparke 112

Lady Eleanor Fuchs 112

Margaret Keep 113

Lady Vaux 114

Mary, Queen of Scots 115

Mrs Graham 116

Queen Henrietta 116

St Werburgh 116

Witches 118

ABOUT THE AUTHORS 121

ACKNOWLEDGEMENTS 121

INTRODUCTION

T HE LADIES OF DISTINCTION represented here may have been famous, infamous or somewhere in between. Their county connections, therefore, are here for a variety of reasons – possibly born in this county, or lived here, or had some influence in their lifetime.

Prior to emancipation, females partaking in business or in feats of 'derring-do' were the exception. In history, women became prominent for a number of reasons, perhaps through birth, marriage, eccentricity, notoriety or stubborn self-promotion.

This 'collection' represents the wide diversity of talent, age and determination to follow a dream, maybe a cause or a calling.

Some gained prominence through doggedness in the face of adversity, or pursuing a burning ambition to succeed, whatever the consequences. Some were very lowly, never seeking exposure, yet playing a vital role in the community, whilst others delight in high profile – such are the whims of women!

Some might be heralded with a fanfare of trumpets, where others more modest would shrink into the dark.

'Cameos' embrace brief notes on an elite coterie of women, of whom it might be said that some, such as Mary Queen of Scots, already have much-recorded history. Conversely, there are others who have scant information available, though these characters are of no less value.

One thing for sure, all here are as diverse as chalk and cheese!

We hope you will be intrigued and inspired by our choices!

Mia Butler
Colin Eaton
2005

*"As for the women, though we scorn
and flout them, we may live with,
but cannot live without them."*

JOHN DRYDEN (1631–1700)

Born at Aldwincle, Northants
Poet Laureate to Charles II

JOAN HICKSON

(1906–1998)

A lady of many parts

To the nation Joan Hickson was the Agatha Christie character 'Miss Marple', the role she played so successfully on BBC Television between 1984 and 1992.

Joan was born on 5 October 1906 in Harborough Road, Kingsthorpe, a village she remembered as a charming place, although at the time of her birth it had already been absorbed into Northampton.

She was first educated at Castle Hall School, a private establishment run by her grandmother, Mrs Bogle, in St Matthew's Parade, a school that Joan regarded as truly excellent, where the children could all read without difficulty before they were five years old.

Her grandfather was a former Justice of the Peace and a prominent shoe manufacturer in Northampton.

Even as a very young girl she wanted to be in show business and become an actress. She would often stand in front of a long mirror in her mother's bedroom with her best hat on back-to-front and prance about; not really knowing what she was doing, probably wanting to show off! She was also in her element when appearing in plays at school.

Her first experience of real theatre came when her parents and grandparents took her to see a pantomime in London called *Cinderella*. She was over-awed by the occasion, especially the transformation scenes, which rendered her speechless. When they got home after the show she remembered saying to her parents that they must move next door to the theatre so that she could go again whenever she wanted.

Her parents had no interest in show business at all and were bewildered why Joan should want to enter the profession: they thought she would grow out of it but, of course, she failed to do so.

The family moved to Ealing during the First World War where she went to junior school but she was not an outstanding pupil – her main interest was putting on plays. She joined the Girl Guides and also took dancing lessons.

The best thing about living in London for her was, of course, being so near to the theatres, and she recalled vividly going to see *Peter Pan* with her aunt and mother. When they told her that Tinkerbell had died, but if everyone in the audience applauded she would come back to life again, Joan put her head down on the back of the seat in front and cried her eyes out. A lady behind asked if the little girl was not enjoying herself, to which her aunt turned round and replied, "We take our pleasures sadly". Joan thought that a wonderful reply and it stayed in her mind for the rest of her life.

At the age of sixteen she went off to boarding school in Swanage, Dorset. It was run by an uncle and aunt from her father's side of the family and was primarily attended by youngsters whose parents were living abroad. It was an unusual school in as much as it was open to boys and girls, so brothers and sisters could be together as often the children would not see their parents for long periods of time.

Following the completion of her education in Dorset, she started to pester her parents about entering show business. They just could not understand Joan's persistence. Her mother would often say, "Oh darling, you're so good with children, why don't you do something with them?". Joan kept up the pressure until one of her uncles intervened and persuaded her parents to allow her to apply to the Royal Academy of Dramatic Art. She auditioned at the age of eighteen and was successful but she had to wait until she was nineteen to actually enroll. In the meantime she worked from home and when she eventually started to study and act for real at RADA, it was 'absolute bliss'.

After two years at the college she won the 'Dion Boucicault' Medal for character parts as well as the 'Academy Diploma'.

In 1927 she made her debut on a provincial tour in a play called *His Wife's Children,* but looking back she admitted she did not think much to it, in fact, "it was an absolute disaster".

The following year she was contracted to two companies run by Beryl Foster and Tom Miller, where she was able to play small parts in a number of plays, usually in the West End of London

She left the capital temporarily between 1931 and 1933 when she joined the Oxford Repertory Theatre where her career blossomed. She had a thorough grounding in the art of 'rep', the company embarking on a new play virtually every week. She thought it wonderful training, an opportunity no longer available to young actors these days.

She always said she was never pretty so she was ideal for character parts. Her first professional part in a tour of the provinces was as a titled lady and her first in a London play was as a maidservant.

She was always able to acquire work playing a host of minor and character roles including prying landladies, dotty aunts, receptionists, charladies and so on. As the Daily Telegraph said in her obituary (19 October 1998): "Few actresses knew better how to keep a large residue of ash on the end of a cigarette in the corner of the mouth while berating (often in a dressing gown) a sullen lodger".

Before the Second World War she was to appear in London in a series of thrillers and a comedy *The Gusher* (Ian Hay). During the War she and her young family were evacuated back to the county where they stayed at Blisworth. During her time there she was often seen giving a helping hand in the YMCA Canteen at the Castle Station in Northampton.

Joan still managed to work a little in London during this time when she appeared in 1944 at The Open Air Theatre in *Lady Precious Stream* and immediately after the War she was Mrs Read in *The Guinea Pig* at The Criterion Theatre.

Her first professional appearance on the stage in her hometown came in February 1945 when she played Miss Pryce, the dithering spinster, in Agatha Christie's *Appointment with Death* at the New Theatre in Abington Street.

Stage parts became fewer as she found work in films. She made her film debut in 1934 in *Widow's Might* and afterwards appeared in such productions as *The Guinea Pig* (1948), *The Million Pound Note* (1953), *Doctor in the House* (1954), *The Thirty-Nine Steps* (1959), *A Day in the Life of Joe Egg* (1970) and *Clockwise* (1985).

She also appeared in five 'Carry On' films, among them *Carry on Nurse* (1959) and *Carry on Regardless* (1961).

Some of her television appearances include *Sinister Street, How to get rid of your Wife, A Murder is Announced* and a serial *Our Man at St Marks*.

Featuring in a hundred or so films, television programmes and hundreds of stage productions – nothing could have prepared her for the celebrity status which was to come her way from 1984. From the first production she became the definitive Miss Marple grabbing up to 15 million viewers for every programme. During the eight-year run she appeared in twelve films and made the part her own. In doing so she became not only a national star, but also an international personality after the series was sold all over the world including Russia and China.

Ironically, when she was first offered the part she turned it down, despite being urged to accept by friends and family, because she thought she was the wrong shape!

When she played in the London run of *Appointment with Death* at the Criterion Theatre, Joan remembered meeting Agatha Christie who she found rather shy and very sweet. Soon after Joan received a letter from Agatha in which the postscript said: "I hope one day you will play my dear Miss Marple". They did not keep in touch and Joan had forgotten all about the letter until one day her daughter Caroline unearthed it when clearing out her mother's writing desk at about the same time of the first television series of Miss Marple.

In 1988 Joan was awarded an honorary Master of Arts degree from Leicester University through what was then Nene College, Northampton. Nicholas her son remembered his mother often speaking with affection about her time in Northampton and her award.

A year earlier an OBE came Joan's way and it was presented to her by Miss Marple's chief fan, the Queen.

Joan was married in 1932 to Eric Butler, a neurologist.

When the show was over, she would get on the train, go home, and become Mrs Butler once more, rather enjoying living two lives. They had two children, a son and a daughter.

Eric died in 1967, from which Joan freely admitted she never recovered, but keeping busy in her profession helped enormously, and further added, "You simply have to go on". She died in a Colchester Hospital, 17 October 1998, and is buried in Devon.

ANNE BRACEGIRDLE

(1671–1748)

Taking London by storm

B ENEATH A MEMORIAL SLAB in the cloisters of Westminster Abbey lie the remains of one of the earliest, most famous and allegedly, a very beautiful actress, Ann Bracegirdle.

Although she was to take London by storm and was known and admired by aristocracy and poor people alike, details of her birthplace and family have been open to conjecture for a very long time.

She was baptised on 15 November 1671 at St Giles Church, Northampton, the daughter of Justinian and Martha Bracegirdle. Her parents had married in All Saints' Church, Northampton, four years earlier; he a gentleman of Creaton, she a spinster of Sibbertoft.

Her tomb gives the date of death as 12 September 1748 and her age as 85, when really she was 77 years old.

Whilst still a child, the family moved to London where her parents put her under the care and tuition of Thomas Betterton, actor, playwright and theatre manager, and his wife.

Anne is said to have made her debut at the age of six (but it is more likely to have been nine) when she took the part of the page in *The Orphan* at the Duke's Theatre in Dorset Gardens.

After playing many minor roles, her talents were first reported in 1688 when she appeared at The Theatre Royal, Drury Lane when she played Lucia in *Squire of Alsatia* by Thomas Shadwell. This was followed by *Edward III* (William Mountford) in which she played Maria, then took the part of Emmeline in John Dryden's *King Arthur*.

One of her friends wrote of her: "She was of a lovely height with dark brown hair and eyebrows, black sparkling eyes and a fresh blushy complexion..."

Courtesy: Chris Covington.

In 1693 she made her first appearance in a comedy as Araminta in *The Old Bachelor*, a part specially written for her by William Congreve in whose later works she was to attain her chief triumphs. Her very close friendship with Congreve was a notorious episode in her life.

When Thomas Betterton opened The Little Theatre in Lincoln's Inn Fields in 1695, Anne played Angelica in *Love for Love*. Two years later she was Almeria in another Congreve play called *Mourning Bride*. Her Shakespeare roles included Isabella in *Measure for Measure*, and Portia in *Merchant of Venice*.

During the 1706/7 season at The Haymarket Theatre, she came into competition with another young actress called Anne Oldfield. Rivalry was fierce between the two, each thinking she was the better performer. To settle the dispute, it was agreed to let the London audiences decide, and so Anne Bracegirdle played Mrs Brittle in Betterton's *Amorous Widow* on one night and Anne Oldfield played the same role on the next night. The outcome was judged to be in favour of Anne Oldfield at which Anne Bracegirdle 'was very much disgusted'. She was also very bitter about Anne Oldfield being allowed to appear at the theatre in the previous season and so she quit the stage immediately!

She refused all offers to return to the platform but did, however, make one last stage appearance in 1709 to take again the role of Angelica in Betterton's *Love for Love*.

Nothing more is heard of Anne Bracegirdle until 18 September 1748, when her body was taken from her house in Howard Street off The Strand and interred in the cloisters at Westminster Abbey.

Like all beautiful women she had many admirers but she was implicated in a celebrated murder trial with an infamous verdict.

A seventeen-year-old nobleman, Lord Mohun, befriended a braggart called Captain Richard Hill. Hill fell in love with Anne and pestered her with his affections, but she spurned him. He suspected a famous actor of the day called William Mountford was the successful rival, so the pair decided to teach him a lesson. A warning message sent by Anne to Mrs Mountford failed to reach her husband. The Mountfords lived in the same street as Anne and on 9 December 1692 the men lay in wait for Mountford and whilst Mohun kept Mounfort talking, Hill came up from behind and stabbed Mountfort in the back. He was treated for his wounds but died the next day.

Hill managed to escape but Mohun was arrested and charged with murder. Parliament was sitting at the time and Lord Mohun chose to be tried by his peers in the House of Lords. He appealed to William III but the king decided to leave it to the judges.

At the trial he was found not guilty by 69 votes to 14. Not one of the 83 lords had any legal training, a fact that caused great consternation among Tories and Whigs and non-jurors who described the result as scandalous. It was generally felt that the blood of the poor had been shed by the great. Witnesses reported the only fair thing about the trial was the show of ladies in the galleries.

Anne's welfare work among the unemployed poor of Clare Market and areas adjacent to her home was evident when it was impossible for her to pass through the neighbourhoods without being acknowledged and universally thanked by all kinds of people. She was able to help these poor folk further by a gift of £800 given to her by the Dukes of Dorset and Devonshire and other noblemen in recognition of her virtuous behaviour.

Although she never married (as far as is known) she was extremely close to the dramatist Richard Congreve who left her a legacy of £200 in his will. Some thought she was secretly married to him.

It was also suspected that Anne had a liaison with Robert Leake, Earl of Scarsdale, but she is remembered in history as a warm-hearted lady and an outstanding actress for her time.

ANNE BRADSTREET

(c.1613–1672)

America's first poetess

ANNE WAS BORN about 1613 into a Puritan family in or near Northampton, the daughter of Thomas Dudley of Yardley Hastings and Dorothy Yorke of Hardingstone.

Her father was first a page to William, Lord Compton, at Castle Ashby, in about 1590, remaining there until 1594 when, at age eighteen, he became clerk to the eminent judge Sir Augustine Nicholls of Faxton. Later still he was appointed steward to the Earl of Lincoln at Semperingham and later at Boston in Lincolnshire.

Thomas had met the celebrated Puritan preacher John Dod and was converted by him in 1597. The Bishop of Oxford dismissed Dod for his preaching of nonconformity but he was able to continue in office at Canons Ashby Church (technically outside the jurisdiction of the Bishop of Oxford) at the invitation of Sir Erasmus Dryden of Canons Ashby House. Here, it is thought, Thomas took Anne to be baptised by Dod in a private ceremony.

Anne's early life was spent in the county but at about the age of seven the family left the undulating landscape of Northamptonshire to go to the flat countryside of the Fens in Lincolnshire. Her education started from the age of about four and continued in various forms until she married in 1628.

Anne did not have a strong constitution; she suffered bouts of illness throughout her life but even so still managed, with a struggle, to raise a family of eight children

The first serious illness occurred when she was twelve. Although it was not identified, she wrote about her symptoms, which included fever, fainting spells and lameness, which probably points to an attack of rheumatic fever that almost certainly damaged her heart and later rendered her vulnerable to collapse if she became over-exerted.

Four years later she wrote in her personal memoirs:

> *About 16, the Lord layd his hand sore upon me and smott me with the small pox. When I was in my affliction, I besought the Lord, and confessed my Pride and Vanity and He was entreated of me, and again restored me...*

In 1621 whilst Anne was engaged in her studies at the family house in Semperingham, a young man arrived in the household, who was destined to be among the founders of New England. His name was Simon Bradstreet, the son of a vicar from a nearby parish and he was employed as Thomas Dudley's assistant.

Three years later Anne's father decided to leave Semperingham and take his family to live in Boston where he could have more independence and, from his position in the town, would be more effective in overall management of the Earl of Lincoln's finances. Simon Bradstreet was left behind to look after the day-to-day running of the estate at Semperingham.

In 1627 the Earl was arrested and committed to prison for refusing to pay the Forced Loan to Charles I.

Anne was coming up to fourteen and must have been aware of the political tensions of the time. She must have also known about the grave danger her father was in, not only because of his religious

Courtesy:
St Botolph's Church,
Boston, Lincs.

9

nonconformity, but also his position of steward to an Earl who had had the audacity to defy the king's orders.

No record of her marriage in 1628 has been found but it is likely that she married Simon Bradstreet at a private ceremony in her parent's house in Boston when she would have been about fifteen years of age. It was thought prudent to hold the service in secret because of a new danger the family was under when Anne's father also defied royal decree by refusing to pay the Forced Loan.

To celebrate the union Anne wrote:

To My Dear and Loving Husband

If ever two were one, then surely we.
If ever man were loved by wife, then thee;
If ever wife was happy in a man,
Compare with me, ye women, if you can.
I prize thy love more than whole mines of gold,
Or all the riches that the East doth hold.
My love is such that rivers cannot quench,
Nor ought but love from thee, give recompense.
Thy love is such I can no way repay;
The heavens reward thee manifold I pray.
Then while we live, in love let's persever,
That when we live no more, we may live ever

A year earlier, a group of Lincolnshire Puritans had sailed to America for fear of their safety in this country and had established the Massachusetts Bay Colony in New England.

Here in England, a new commercial company was formed called The Massachusetts Bay and those members who intended to emigrate, including the Dudleys and the Bradstreets, assembled for departure in April 1630.

The flagship of the fleet was the *Arbella* on which Anne and her parents, husband and brother and sisters sailed. Leaving her childhood behind in England and reinforced by her faith, she looked forward, with her family, to a new life and new challenges.

The journey was not an easy one, much stormy weather was encountered, with rain and fog interspersed with days of calm. Uncomfortable quarters, the prevailing cold, a diet of salt meat and hard biscuits, are some of the things the passengers had to endure.

They eventually set foot in New England on 12 June after sixty-six days at sea. Anne wrote in her memoirs:

I... came into this Country, where I found a new world and new manners, At which my heart rose. But after I was convinced it was the way of God, I Submitted to it and joined the church at Boston.

After the normal life she had led in England, it took her quite some time to come to terms with the primitive colonial existence she had been brought into, where there was dirt, overcrowding, hastily-built shelters, diseases, homesickness and discouragement.

In the spring of the following year, the Bradstreets and Dudleys were given house-lots at a new settlement a few miles up the Charles River called Newtown in which they were able to live much more comfortably in sturdy housing.

During the second year at Newtown, Anne again fell ill and, after recovering, wrote the following poem. It is one of the earliest examples of her writing in verse:

Upon a Fit of Sickness, Anno 1632

Twice ten years old, not fully told
Since nature gave me breath,
My race is run, my thread is spun,
Lo here is fatal death.
All men must dye, and so must I
This cannot be revok'd
For Adams sake, this word God spake
When so high provok'd.
Yet live I shall, this life's but small,
In peace of highest bliss,
Where I shall have all I can crave,
No life is like to this.
For what's this life, but care and strife?
Since first we came from womb,
Our strength doth waste, our time doth haste,
And then we go to th' Tomb...

In 1640 was published her volume of verse called *Several Poems*. It must have been a tremendous thrill for Anne when she was able, for the first time, to actually hold in her hands the small book of her own work.

Anne's brother-in-law, John Woodbridge, apparently without her consent or knowledge, took the poems to England where they were published under the title *The Tenth Muse Lately Sprung Up in America*.

Simon and Anne meanwhile, had to wait six years for the birth of their first child, Samuel in 1634. She wrote in her diary:

> *It pleased God to keep me a long time without child, which was a great Greif to me, and cost mee many prayers and tears before I obtained one, And after him gave mee many more.*

Anne and Simon were to have seven more children born between 1635 and 1652 – she being fertile despite her spells of ill health.

> *I had eight birds hatcht in one nest,*
> *Four cocks there were and hens the rest.*

Anne and her family, along with her parents, moved house again in 1635, this time to a place on the coast about forty miles north of the Charles River called Ipswich.

In July 1653, Anne's father died in his seventy-seventh year. He had been the principal founder and second Governor of the colony and had never been out of the magistracy, and had been either Governor or deputy.

Anne missed her father terribly and in her sorrowing wrote the following:

> *My mournful mind*
> *Presents my Lamentations at His Herse,*
> *Who was my Father, Guide, Instructor too,*
> *To whom I ought what ever I could doe:*
>
> *Let malice bite, and envy know its full,*
> *He was my Father, and Ile praise him still.*
> *Well known and lov'd, where'ere he lived, by most*
> *Both in his native, and in foreign coast...*

In 1666 the family home suffered a disastrous fire when the house and most of the contents were lost. It must have been heartbreaking for Anne and Simon to begin all over again, especially for Anne who was in her mid-fifties with failing health, bereft of books and left with only the barest household utensils. The following verses illustrate how she felt:

> *In silent night when rest I took*
> *For sorrow neer I did not look,*
> *I wakened was with thund'ring noise*
> *And pitious shreiks of dreadful voice.*

That fearfull sound of fire and fire,
Let no man know is my desire.
I, starting up, ye light did spy,
And to my God my heart did cry
To strengthen me in my Distresse
And not to leave me succourlesse...

Although she was to live another three years, Anne wrote in 1669 her farewell to the earth. The poem is the only one that survives in her own handwriting:

In weakness and dishonour sowne
in power 'tis rais'd by Christ alone
Then soule and body shall unite
And of their maker have the sight
Such lasting joys, shall there behold
As eare ner' heard nor tongue e'er told
Lord make me ready for that day
then come deare bridegroom come away

Anne Bradstreet, who had helped to create another England and had laid the foundations of literary America with her mind and hand, died 16 September 1672 at the age of about 59. No gravestone marks her final resting-place but it is likely to have been in an old burial ground not far from where the family home stood in Andover.

In his book *The Elizabethans and America*, A L Rowse, referring to literary qualities wrote: "...what a story they had to write! Then shortly, after winter, they would be putting forth shoots of poetry, naïve, musical, delightful as a birdsong with Anne Bradstreet".

Leonard Bernstein in his 'Songfest' set her poem *To my Dear and Loving Husband* to music in 1976.

A VERY PERSONAL CHANCE ENCOUNTER

An extraordinary coincidence occurred, quite by chance, at a Champagne Reception, which took place on a warm June evening in Newburyport, Massachusetts, U.S.A.

The author (Mia) was attending this function – a book-signing on Gardens of the New Republic and wandered off to seek a breath of sea air and lean in the doorway of the crowded hall. No doubt, also taking a whiff of the evening breeze, I spoke to an elderly lady picking at a plate of succulent strawberries dipped in chocolate, glass in hand and, as is usual at such gatherings, nowhere to set either down!

I asked what her interests might be, aside from gardening, and she was happy to launch into her favourite subject, America's first female poet. She regaled me with the fascinating story of a plucky young Puritan woman who had sailed from England with her family to Massachusetts in the 17th century. Many such groups had braved the hazards of the long Atlantic voyage and the vast unknown territory of the North American continent.

After a few moments, there was a flicker in my memory and I interrupted to ask, "Are you talking about Ann Bradstreet?"

She took a sharp intake of breath, her eyes widened and lit up.

"How would you, an English woman, know about Ann Bradstreet?" she enquired.

A good question, for it so happened that, *The Tenth Muse* was already on the list and indeed, in my current file for the next book! The subject had been born in this county of local parents.

Nancy Weare, as she introduced herself, asked for my 'phone number, actually that of my host with whom I was staying, in fact, an old school friend from my home town, where together we had attended a little private school at the age of five. (But *that* is another story!).

This charming lady called that same evening and arranged to take us both to Ipswich, whose original name was Agawam, 30 miles north of the city of Boston, a prosperous town blessed with a number of surviving First Period homes, some as early as 1625. This coastal community was first settled in 1633 and consequently, rich in American history.

It transpired we had passed along this beautiful tree-lined High Street many times before on the way to our favourite Cranes Beach, an enchanting four-mile stretch of white sand backed by impressive dunes. We had perused the painted boards on some of these striking homes, telling of their proud heritage and previous residents.

However, we had missed the handsome bronze plaque fixed to a massive granite block at street level, marking the nearby site of the home of Simon Bradstreet, Governor of Massachusetts Bay 1679–1686 and 1689–1692, whose wife, Ann, daughter of Governor

Plaque at Ipswich: Mia Butler.

Dudley, was the first American poetess. They had lived in Ipswich from 1636–1644, with their burgeoning family.

We then took a short journey to North Andover, to the Stevens Memorial Library, where Nancy requested access to the Ann Bradstreet Collection of publications and documents, which were brought from safe-keeping, for our perusal. Also here, a personal treasure is secreted; a small-sheepskin bound notebook in which Ann penned her poems and thoughts, dated in her own handwriting 20 March 1664.

Toward evening, we drove to the Old Churchyard, seemingly neglected yet with a certain elegance, though no church. Anne is known to have lived within half a mile of this place, though her precise grave is not identified. I sat on the grass in this isolated spot, among the ageing gravestones, reflecting on her life and gazed at the handsome commemorative headstone, set apart beneath the towering larch and chestnut trees, recording the following:

Courtesy: Mia Butler.

Anne Dudley Bradstreet
1612–1672
Mirror of Her Age, Glory of her Sex
whose heaven-born Soul
leaving its earthly Shrine,
chose its native home
and was taken to its Rest
upon 16th September 1672.

John Norton Jr 1672

I pondered on the sombre gathering for the funeral, visualising these gentle people whose absolute faith had driven them to a new land. They now mourned the loss of a respected member of their religious band of pilgrims.

I pictured the mourning clothes, the pious ladies clad in long gowns whose hems swept the grass, worn with crisp white caps and the dark suits of the gentlemen with round black hats, some heavily bearded.

I could see the people drifting, ghost-like, in this hushed setting, which has changed little in 400 years.

Would there have been horses to haul the simple coffin or would the bier have rested on a handcart? Might there have been a burial service at the graveside? Maybe hymns were sung or would the subdued folk move quietly following the cortege, to pay their respects? Would the dignified members of the Puritan community file past the grave in reverent silence? A much-loved pillar of their society, with strong family connections, would surely leave a void among them.

In the closing chapter of her book of days, Anne left us with a wealth of words of wisdom. One of her Meditations is quoted here:

> *To My Dear Children*
>
> *This book by any yet unread,*
> *I leave for you when I am dead,*
> *That being gone, so you may find*
> *What was your living mother's mind.*
> *Make use of what I leave in love,*
> *And God shall bless you from above.*

As we drove away, leaving the Stars and Stripes fluttering against the setting sun, in this almost forgotten oasis of tranquillity, I wondered, on the other hand, of what fate had steered me toward Nancy Weare, this knowledgeable lady, in a throng of more than a hundred people.

Nancy has produced an exquisite booklet, *Anne Bradstreet, America's First Poet*, illustrating this sensitive work, which she gave to me as a gift of remembrance. I was touched by the kindly gesture and feel privileged to have been in her company, which enabled me to add a very personal note to this chapter, in celebration of a Puritan gentlewoman from this county of Northamptonshire.

Mia

BERNICE FIELD

(1900–1963)

The Merry Comrades' Leader

AT THE AGE of 19, Bernice entered the world of journalism after the First World War. Along with her usual newspaper work, she compiled and edited a weekly column for children. This column resulted in the beginning of a crusade in which she was eventually able to help make the life of children a little better whether they were in hospital, had disabilities or were underprivileged. Over the years she was also instrumental in helping the elderly in care as well as members of the armed forces in times of war.

Bernice Mary Power was born on 25 October 1900 in the parish of St Giles, Northampton, the daughter of Walter and Julia Hay. Julia was a teacher who founded the Farringdon Preparatory School in the St James area of Northampton.

1919, Bernice was one of the earliest women journalists.

After leaving school, she became one of the first provincial women journalists, working as a young reporter on the Northampton Daily Echo. From the outset she showed great promise in a job that previously had been an all male preserve. She was soon approached by the Editor of the sister paper, the weekly Northampton Mercury, with a proposal that she write a weekly letter aimed at boys and girls to include stories, competitions and the setting up of a club.

Before the First World War there used to be a similar column for children called *The Uncle Dick Society* which was conducted by a member of staff. It had to be abandoned during the war years because of the scarcity of newsprint, and Uncle Dick had since emigrated to Australia.

She was asked to choose a pseudonym for her new column and, no doubt, surprised both editor and staff by opting for 'Auntie Dick'. The chosen name was, however, not unique as Bernice almost certainly noticed when reading through the archive editions of previous Uncle Dick Society columns. Children, when writing to Uncle Dick, often began their letters with 'Dear Uncle and Auntie Dick'.

Auntie Dick's first children's column appeared on 21 November 1919 entitled 'The Merry Comrades' Circle – Conducted by Auntie Dick'. She urged all young readers to fill in the form and become members, promising in future editions there would be 'jolly competitions, good stories, riddles, games and other things'.

There were only two rules to abide by in the Circle: 1) boys and girls must be under sixteen years of age; 2) all those who joined must be kind to birds and animals and help one another.

As well as conducting the children's corner, Bernice carried on her job as a reporter and was sent one day to interview Edward Field who had recently joined the teaching staff at Northampton Grammar School for Boys in Billing Road. It turned out not to be the usual run-of-the-mill assignment for a young, good-looking lady reporter – for they married in 1924 and eventually had two sons, Michael and Richard. Dr Field later became Deputy Headmaster, a post he held for twenty-four years prior to retirement in 1951.

After her marriage she gave up full-time journalism and carried on her work with the Merry Comrades mainly from her home. In addition to the competitions, stories, lists of the names and addresses of the new members and their birthdays, Bernice wrote a weekly 'Auntie Dick's Letter' in which she related such items as the antics of her dog 'Billy'. He often got into all sorts of mischief including the time he ran off to her old home after she and her husband had moved into a new house. When her sons were born, she kept the members of the Merry Comrades informed of their progress.

From early on Auntie Dick wanted her Merry Comrades' Circle to have a purpose rather than be just a weekly entertainment column of competitions and stories. Her opportunity came in 1932 when two Northampton weekly newspapers, the Mercury and the Herald combined to form the Mercury and Herald. Auntie Dick proposed, with

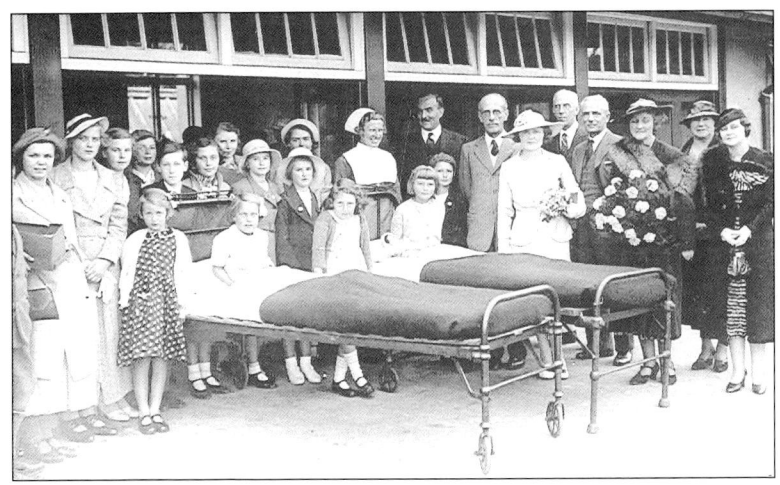

1937; Auntie Dick (centre, in light suit) at the presentation of the first Merry Comrades' Cot to Manfield Hospital, Northampton.

the help of the Merry Comrades, to raise money for the benefit of children unfortunate enough to be in hospital. The hospitals concerned were to be within the area where the Mercury and Herald was circulated. This, of course, was in the days before the advent of the National Health Service. The new managing editor was in full agreement with Auntie Dick's ideas, and actively encouraged her.

With so many girls and boys becoming new members, Auntie Dick decided to give them a good cause to work for and reminded them to think of others less fortunate than themselves. The project decided upon was to be called the Cot Fund. The Merry Comrades were set a target of raising £500 to endow a cot at Manfield Hospital, Northampton. In those days £500 was an enormous amount and bearing in mind the Merry Comrades had never before raised money for charity, progress was rather slow.

Directed by Auntie Dick, with the aid of adult helpers, money was raised in various ways including competitions, bring-and-buy sales, collecting boxes, whist drives, saving silver paper (to be sold later) and charity functions. Merry Comrade Stewart Adams of Byfield came up with a suggestion of selling scented greetings cards which, over the years, proved to be a very successful venture.

The time taken to raise the required amount for that first project was five years. On 30 June 1937, a red letter day for the Merry Comrades, a cheque for the £500 to endow the cot was presented to Manfield

Hospital by Auntie Dick and was officially known as 'The Merry Comrades Cot'.

The next big project was to raise £600 for a similar cot in the Children's Ward at Northampton General Hospital. Raising cash for children in hospital proved a great attraction and many more new members were enrolled. Consequently, fund raising became a little easier and the £600 was collected in four years.

Auntie Dick suggested many different ways in which children could collect money for the good causes. For instance, any child who helped to raise £1 during the year became a 'captain', and those who raised such money themselves in coinage such as farthings, ship halfpennies or bun pennies became 'star captains'. They all received a badge, which rewarded that year's effort. (Some older Merry Comrades were proud to display as many as half a dozen or more 'captain' or 'star captain' badges on their coats). At Christmas time they were invited to special performances of the annual pantomime at the New Theatre, Northampton and when that closed down in 1958, at the Royal Theatre in the town.

In the weeks leading up to Christmas Auntie Dick would ask members to send her any toys, books, games and dolls etc., so that children in Dr. Barnardo's Home, disabled youngsters, those in hospital and the very poor children in official Scattered Homes could all have a Christmas present. In 1936 one whole room in Auntie Dick's house was crammed full of these welcome gifts.

1937, Auntie Dick (centre) at the first Merry Comrades' Sale.

From 1937 Auntie Dick organised annual egg collections, mainly from the village branches, where Merry Comrades called at houses and farms asking for eggs to be donated for children in hospital. In April of that year 3,321 eggs were sent for the young patients in Manfield Hospital.

It was also decided to hold a yearly Merry Comrades' Christmas Bazaar where branches could have stalls to sell items and there would also be competitions and the like. The first bazaar was held at the Dover Hall, St James, Northampton where £140 was made which was donated to Northampton General Hospital.

As the Christmas Bazaars became more popular, larger venues were needed and so the Drill Hall and the Guildhall, both in Northampton, were regularly used. The profit from the last event organised by Auntie Dick in 1962 was in excess of £1,550.

Every year after the Christmas holidays, Auntie Dick reminded the members to save all their Christmas cards so that the old centres could be removed and new printed ones pasted in their place enabling them to be resold.

During the Second World War the Merry Comrades turned their attention to providing comforts for fighting men. From limited resources of wool, members and adult helpers began knitting squares which were eventually stitched together to make blankets. These were given to the British Red Cross to be distributed to British prisoners of war. Money was also raised to send food parcels, cigarettes, books and clothes to men of the Northamptonshire Regiment who were held in Germany.

Auntie Dick also suggested that some of the Merry Comrades, particularly in the rural areas, might like to organise gardening squads in order to cultivate allotments of land to grow vegetables and fruit to help alleviate the National Shortage. Her request, this time, fell on deaf ears.

A much more successful idea to raise money, however, was when Auntie Dick formed her own concert party during the early years of the war. The Auntie Dick Concert Party toured the villages entertaining audiences, which generated money for Merry Comrades Funds. Taking part were girl dancers of varying shapes, height and ability, Wally the conjuror, an elderly storyteller, a male singer and a soloist who played music on a wood-cutting saw. Merry Comrade branches up and down the county eagerly looked forward to visits of the concert party, which was always led by Auntie Dick.

In 1944 money was provided to purchase a radio set for the

Gynaecological Ward and the Children's Ward, both at Northampton General Hospital and the Children's Ward at Manfield Hospital.

The returning prisoners of war were not forgotten by the Merry Comrades. Each one, who lived in the area where the Mercury and Herald was circulated, was entitled to a cheque for two guineas (£2.10p). By the end of July 1944, over five hundred ex-prisoners of war had received their welcome home present.

After the war, fund-raising continued and by November 1947 enough money had been raised to provide every bed in Northampton General Hospital as well as the Margaret Spencer Convalescent Home in Dallington, with a radio and headphones. Fifty extra headphones had also been presented to cover any breakages. They started with a target of £1,000, but as time went on, prices increased until eventually the total cost rose to £2,000. To mark the celebration, a party at Northampton Town Hall was organised and Auntie Dick invited all the members who had raised at least £1 towards the cost. Two oak plaques, which were to be placed in the main halls of both buildings commemorating the gifts, were presented to Earl Spencer. Following the ceremony a variety show was performed which included dancers, a ventriloquist, marionettes, impressionist and instrumentalists.

The next major project in 1948 was to raise £500 to provide a small bathing pool for Manfield Hospital to allow the children with polio and other physical disabilities to strengthen their muscles through exercise under the water. Previously the young patients had been taken to the indoor pool in Northampton for their workout. With £400 being made at the Merry Comrades' Christmas Sale that year, a cheque for £600 was presented to the hospital in March 1949.

The following year saw a change to the name of the radio fund. In future it was to be known as 'The Merry Comrades Radio and Comforts Fund' where items other than radios would be provided where there was a need. One of the first examples was the provision of twelve garden chairs for the residents of Darsdale Home for the Blind at Raunds.

In the 1950s comics and magazines were collected and sorted and then sent to children as well as adults who were in hospital. There was another drive to save metal bottle tops, silver paper, old newspapers and old greetings cards, which could all be resold to raise more much needed cash.

The Merry Comrades' membership surged during this period, so much so, that Auntie Dick had to employ an assistant to open all the incoming parcels at the Merry Comrades office.

The annual egg collection in spring continued unabated. In April 1957 the number of eggs collected and presented to hospitals was 18,169. In 1958: 21,276; 1959: 27,748; 1960: 20,000; 1961: 25,173 and in 1962: 27,000.

Nearing the tenth anniversary of the installation of radio at Northampton General Hospital, it was decided to upgrade the system in order to include a choice of two radio programmes for the patients. The cost was £2,700, which was raised in the usual manner. On 11 April 1958 in the Nurse's Home at Northampton General Hospital, in the presence of Earl Spencer, were 200 helpers and leaders of the Merry Comrades who had come from all parts of Northamptonshire and North Buckinghamshire. To mark the commemoration of handing over the new radio system, Auntie Dick presented to the Earl a Merry Comrades Hospital Autograph Book which contained the names of the leaders and parents who had arranged functions to accumulate the cash and the names of hundreds of boys and girls who had helped in the raising of that money.

Auntie Dick said: "It shows how much the children love to help people in hospitals."

Earl Spencer, in a tribute to Auntie Dick declared: "She is the mainspring from which all this good work has emanated. I should like to offer millions of congratulations to her for the way she has managed the Merry Comrades for so many years and for all the successes she has attained."

The new radio system comprised 334 headphones for wards with two or more beds as well as 154 loudspeakers. Also included was the Barratt Maternity Home, which had previously been without any radio facilities. During the life of the old system the Merry Comrades had been entirely responsible for repairing and maintaining it.

In the summer of 1959, Auntie Dick thought it a good idea to reward the dedication shown by the adult helpers by organising a coach trip to London where they saw a performance of *My Fair Lady*. This outing became an annual event.

In July 1961 the next major project for the Merry Comrades was to raise £1,800 for a hydrotherapy bathing pool for the John Shipman Home in Dallington for children with polio and other physical handicaps. Previously, the children had to be taken by road to use the pool supplied by the Merry Comrades at Manfield Hospital in 1949.

In less than two years the Merry Comrades had raised all the money and Auntie Dick arranged for the new pool to be officially handed over to the John Shipman Home by Jackie Enfield, the famous swimmer from Northampton. It turned out to be the last big fund raising event organised by Auntie Dick.

In addition to all the big fund-raising efforts, Auntie Dick also counted all the farthings, halfpennies and pennies that the children sent in, prior to banking them. She sorted all the silver paper and metal bottle tops and renovated the used Christmas cards. Keeping a close eye on the Merry Comrades' cots, she made sure any new young patient was properly welcomed and gave them little presents. To make sure the members knew all about them, she included their names, where they were from and their progress, in her weekly letter in the Mercury and Herald. In addition to her very busy life, she was a member of Schools Boards of Managers and several local Hospital Committees.

In the summer of 1962, in recognition of the sterling work over the years, she was invited to a garden party at Buckingham Palace.

During 1963 television sets were presented to Park Hospital, Wellingborough; the Children's Ward in Highfield Convalescent Home also in Wellingborough and Rushden Sanatoriums.

By the time of her early death in 1963, Bernice Field had been Auntie Dick for forty-four years and had nurtured and reared a unique children's organisation which had, over time, raised tens of thousands of pounds for very many good causes.

Reporting her death, the Mercury and Herald stated: "Her gracious personality radiated the joy in service and giving she sought so successfully to inculcate, and made her the cherished leader of a children's circle without parallel in the United Kingdom, if, indeed the world."

At her funeral service on 3 October 1963 in St Matthew's Church, Northampton, the Vicar of St Giles, Northampton said: "There is not a word of mercy, not a service which has not been done during these past years which has not been adorned and gilded by the special gifts of Mrs Field."

Some of the tributes to Auntie Dick that poured into the offices of the Mercury and Herald included the following:

Mr L W Dickens, Editor of the Mercury and Herald:

> *"She gave a lifetime of service to helping those in need and it was the privilege of the Mercury and Herald to sponsor that work."*

M W Cowper Barrons, former Managing Editor of the Chronicle & Echo:

> *"...for thirty years as her collaborator, Auntie Dick amazed me by her devotion, her energy – and her modesty."*

Mr S Kilsby, Chairman of the House Committee of St. Edmund's, Welford Road and Harborough Road Hospitals:

> *"Her life's work was devoted to working for others. She was vital, and was able to pass on to others the joy and happiness she had herself."*

Mr S G Hill, Superintendent, Northampton General Hospital and Secretary of Northampton District Hospital Management Committee:

> *"Hospitals throughout this area have lost a warm-hearted and generous friend who has been responsible for the provision of substantially, all the amenities particularly radio and television, in all hospitals and many similar establishments."*

As the Northampton Independent stated in her obituary in November 1963: "If Mrs. Bernice Field had been the subject of a *This is your Life* programme, the BBC would have been embarrassed by the volume of witnesses to her work on behalf of hospitals and all in trouble".

If ever a person deserved to be officially recognised for her years of devoted public service, Bernice Field was that person. A civil honour would have been a fitting tribute to this hard working, dedicated and charismatic lady.

FOOTNOTE

Bernice's two sons, Michael and Richard, both followed her into journalism. Michael became Deputy Editor of the Chronicle & Echo, Northampton before moving on to work for other newspapers. He died in Sheffield in 1994. Richard was editor of the Mercury & Herald from 1965 to 1972 before moving into newspaper management in the North of England. He now lives in North Yorkshire.

Their father, Dr E E Field, died in 1961.

BERTHA WILLMOTT

(1895–1973)

Mine hostess with a voice

BERTHA STARTED SINGING at an early age and was helped to perfect it by nuns. Entering into show business, she worked her way up through the profession from minor beginnings, to reach national recognition with a top-selling song.

She was born on 16 September 1895 at East Ham in the East End of London. Her family were Catholics and young Bertha was educated at a convent school where the nuns witnessed the remarkable things she could do with her voice and encouraged her to develop it.

Later she surprised her family by wanting to go on the stage to sing for a living and after leaving the convent school, they allowed her to study at the London College of Music where she further improved her singing prowess.

Her first public performance, using the name of Little Molly, was at an East Ham cinema when she sang *Heroes of the Mine* written in 1909, and she was assisted in her song by the use of lantern slides projected onto the screen.

She joined and toured with a number of concert parties of which 'The Poppies' was probably the most successful. She soon became known in the provinces appearing in working men's clubs and the like, as an Irish colleen entertaining her audiences with good old Irish airs sung in costume.

In 1914 she decided to stop using the name Little Molly and reverted back to her real name. It was in March of that year that she first came to Northamptonshire when she appeared at the Rushden Working Men's Club where her fee was £1.15s.0d (£1.75p).

She made return visits to the county when she appeared in working men's clubs in Northampton, Irthlingborough, Kettering and Wellingborough.

Later in 1914 she appeared in a show called *Razzle Dazzle* at the Theatre Royal, Drury Lane, London and afterwards decided to concentrate her talents into musical comedy.

She continued her performances at working men's clubs and during the First World War took part in several shows, mostly as a chorus singer, entertaining the troops home on leave.

At the end of the war Bertha married Reginald Seymour, a native of Kent, who worked for J Lyons and Co. in their hotel business. They had one son, Donald, who was born in 1920.

It was about this time Bertha joined the Concert Artists' Association in London, from whom she received most offers of work. Thereafter followed bookings at Masonic halls, after-dinner engagements and summer shows at coastal resorts.

With the introduction of radio in the early 1920s, she was invited to take part in one of the first broadcasts on the BBC's 2LO station at their studios in Savoy Hill, London. She was billed as the 'Radio Girl with a Voice' and an acclaimed successor of legendary former music hall star Marie Lloyd.

Courtesy: Nancy Seymour.

Bertha had the ability to project her voice, if needed, to reach the back of the gallery without the use of a microphone. Her first radio engagement was a success and she was to take part in many other broadcasts including *Henry Hall's Guest Night* and *Old Music Hall* in which she appeared with Tessa Dean, Denis O'Neil, John Rourke and the BBC Revue Orchestra conducted by Stanford Robinson. The public took her to their hearts and in 1933 she was proclaimed 'Radio Star of the Year'.

It was during one of her Music Hall shows that she first introduced and sang a new song called *Roll out the Barrel* which became a huge success on both sides of the Atlantic. Published in 1934 it was originally called *Beer Barrel Polka* or *Czecho-Slovakian Polka* and was based on the European success of that year called *Skoda Lasky*. It was the song with which she was associated for the rest of her life.

To help her remember the words of new songs, Bertha would write them out on a large sheet of paper and pin it up in her lounge, kitchen or bedroom so she could memorise them for future performances.

Apart from her work in radio and on the stage, she appeared in two films, *Variety* (1935) in which she sang with Billy Cotton and his Band and *Millions Like Us* (1943). This portrayed the life of a young lady (Patricia Roc) who left her home during the Second World War to work in an aircraft-engineering factory and met an RAF pilot (Gordon Jackson) who was later killed. Bertha sang two songs, *Just Like the Ivy* and *Waiting at the Church*.

Reg, Bertha's husband, who had been promoted to manager of the Cumberland Hotel in London, had become ill with a chest complaint and was advised to move out of London. After talks with a Northampton brewery, Reg and Bertha became licensees of The Spinney Hill public house on Kettering Road in the town.

In 1939 she was one of the first entertainers to join ENSA (Entertainments National Service Association) and in November of that year accompanied Sir Seymour Hick's first company to entertain troops of the British Expeditionary Force in France.

She appeared with a number of variety stars of the day including Billy Russell, Jimmy Blades, dancers 'The Ascots' and wartime cartoonist Tom Webster.

They performed in theatres, picture houses as well as under canvas. Bertha recalled that at three separate venues, when she went on stage, a cry went up: "Good Old Spinney" and "Up the Cobblers" (nickname of Northampton Town Football Club) a lump came in her throat which she found very difficult to control. During that tour she also showed her prowess at darts. She had asked early on if someone could produce a dartboard, which was obtained, and from then on proceeded to beat everyone who challenged her.

If she wanted the music of any particular song transposed to a key suitable for the range of her voice, a good friend Dick Brewster, leader of a Northampton dance band, would spend an evening at 'The Spinney' and carry out the work for Bertha.

She carried on her wartime engagements from her new home in Northampton which included a regular Friday evening radio programme at 6.30pm called *Your Cup of Tea*. It was broadcast on the BBC Empire Service to British forces from a studio in Portland Place, London, and sent over the airways to Africa and the Middle East from the BBC transmitters on Borough Hill, overlooking Daventry, in this county.

Mothers, wives, sweethearts and friends of troops serving abroad were invited to the studio to send messages to their loved ones. Bertha sang during the show, accompanied by pianist Billy Mayerl and at the end of each broadcast, the guests in the studio gathered round the piano to join in the chorus of Bertha's last offering.

A regular visitor to 'The Spinney' during the latter part of the Second World War was American heart-throb Clarke Gable who came down from his air base in the north of the county. His visits (although secret) always attracted large numbers of people to the pub (news travelled fast in those days).

Her first appearance of many at the New Theatre, Northampton, occurred in 1932 when she shared bottom billing with lifetime friend Ben Warris in a show called *Ridgeway Parade*. Twenty-six years later she was campaigning to keep the theatre open as audiences declined because of the impact of television. All the hard work was to no avail, however, as the last-ever show *Strip, Strip, Hooray* finished on 16 August 1958 and the building, which then stood empty for some time, was finally demolished in 1960.

She joined the Grand Order of Lady Ratlings in the 1940s, a show business charitable organisation, and became Queen Ratling for the year 1953 when her friend Ben Warris was elected King Rat.

Her last stage appearance was at the Adelphi Theatre, London in 1953 in a show with the Lady Ratlings.

Her hobbies included horse riding, golf, darts and above all fishing. Coarse fishing usually but she much preferred fishing in the sea.

Her health deteriorated in the late 1950s and, after a serious operation in 1959, finally gave up show business. Husband Reg died in

1962 and she decided to retire from the licensing trade and moved into a house in Grendon Walk, Spinney Hill, Northampton, where she spent the rest of her retirement.

She was able to keep up with the happenings in show business with visits from her many friends including Ben Warris, Charlie Chester and Billy Cotton.

She became seriously ill in 1973 and was admitted to Northampton General Hospital where she died on 3 June.

Bertha could have made herself more successful internationally had she undertaken lengthy tours of the then British Empire and America but she preferred not to be away too long from her home and family. She was quite content in her married life, to help run the public house and have two weeks holiday with her family in the summer of every year.

On being asked how she looked upon her theatrical career, she replied: "It's been a full life and I've enjoyed it". A fitting tribute to a memorable personality.

CAROLINE BRADLEY

(1946–1983)

Show jumper extraordinaire

C AROLINE, a post World War Two baby, grew up with and spent all of her life with horses. When she chose show jumping as her full time occupation, she worked at it with determination and style, eventually reaching the very top. She was a very private person and shunned the publicity spotlight. In her relatively short life, however, she became the best lady show jumper the country has ever produced.

Born in April 1946 and registered in the Oxford District, she was born into a comfortably off but by no means wealthy family. Father Tom was a county land agent for Northamptonshire and valuer who had relatively little experience of horses. Mother Doreen, on the other hand, came from farming stock, was a keen foxhunter and brought a fine hunter into their marriage. Both parents were keen sports people – both enjoyed tennis and Tom also liked to play cricket and rugby (not the Saints).

Caroline's elder sister Judith inherited a pony, but as soon as Caroline was able to walk, and in order to keep the peace, Tom went off in search of a suitable pony for his younger daughter.

From her earliest times Caroline was infatuated with horses and neither child needed any encouragement to ride – their attraction to horses had been passed down through genes from Doreen's side of the family.

An early pony Tom bought Caroline, costing £15, was a 3-year-old Anglo-Arab standing at 14.2 hh. Although she initially had some teething troubles the first time she took it hunting, it settled down and, with her training and influence, the pair enjoyed a number of successes in Pony Club events.

In those early days there was no horse transport. If Caroline wanted to take part in any particular event, she would have to get up at dawn, prepare the horse and then ride to the venue and return in the same manner.

Caroline's unusual affinity to horses allowed her to sense what any particular horse found difficult and was uncomfortable with, as well as knowing when they were confident and happy in any situation giving her the ability to get the best out of her animals.

All of the horses and ponies that Caroline purchased were uneducated. She brought them on to a very high standard which attracted buyers from far and near when it was selling time.

She attended Northampton High School for Girls and as well as doing well in her schoolwork, she showed and enjoyed an interest in sport, particularly hockey in which she was very successful. At that time she thought she might like to become a physical education teacher when she left school, but in the end she plumped for the world of equitation.

Her first significant success in the saddle was with her second horse called Ivanovitch. Bred in Russia, it did not come up to the expectations of the owner and was put on the market. After weighing up its potential on a test ride, Caroline was in no doubt about its ability and purchased it for £50. Under her hand she brought it on to an 'A' grade international horse.

After leaving school she went for riding instruction at the school run by the Swedish teacher Lars Sederholm at Waterstock near Thame in Oxfordshire, where she stayed for eighteen months as a working pupil. After telling her tutor that she wanted to be taught properly and with no short cuts, she was to endure a gruelling time but never complained or left before the end of the course. The training she received under Sederholm was instrumental in achieving her just rewards in show jumping.

Having been brought up at The Old Vicarage in Pattishall, where the family lived from 1954 until 1971, she was soon winning competitions at local shows including Northampton Borough Council's Town Show at Abington Park, the British Timken Show at Duston and the Cross Country Horse Trials at Everdon Hall.

Whilst riding Ivanovitch, she was spotted by Robert Hanson who was so inspired by her style and verve, he offered to let her ride his horse Franco, which had previously been ridden by David Barker in the 1960 Olympics.

In 1966 she made her international debut at Dublin with the British Team, taking with her Franco and Ivanovitch where she won two speed classes.

The following year she competed in the North American circuit and on Franco won the Civilian Open Championship at the Toronto Winter Fair in Canada. Later she was beaten into second place at the New York Grand Prix by Harvey Smith.

Her successes were now attracting the media. Interviews for radio, television, newspapers and magazines were beginning to become every day events. Although she knew that she was a public figure and had, to some extent, to oblige the reporters, interviewers and photographers, it was something she tolerated but was never entirely at ease.

The early 1970s were a relatively quiet time for Caroline. Towards the middle of the decade she bought, in partnership with a Midlands businessman, a German Hanoverian thoroughbred called Tigre. The horse had previously been described as unrideable but Caroline, in her inimitable manner, got the very best out of him. Indeed, she was probably the first woman ever to sit astride him.

In October 1977 she bounced back in *The Horse of the Year Show* at Wembley. Pitted against the leading riders of the world, she virtually swept the board. On that memorable Wednesday night, she won the Leading Show Jumper of the Year on Marius, was joint second on Berna as well as fourth place on her latest acquisition Tigre.

Her next aim was a place in the British Team for the World Championships at Aachen in 1978. Her horses had been well prepared during the winter of 1977/78 and, of course, she was over the moon when she knew she had been picked. Alongside Caroline, the team consisted of David Broome, Malcolm Pyrah and Derek Ricketts. That year the Championships were run under new open rules, which meant that Caroline was the first woman rider to compete against the men.

During the first round she had a minor disaster by having three fences down and, to say she was disappointed, was an understatement. In the team rounds on the following day, she rode Tigre into that impressive ring and in front of an audience of 42,000, really showed the British flag by jumping two of the very best clear rounds of her life. It was Caroline's outstanding performances, which clinched the gold medal for the British team, making them the best in the world.

During the following year she had successes in the Nice Grand Prix, the Calgary Grand Prix in Canada, as well as helping the British team win the European Title on Tigre.

In 1980 she was again in winning form on Tigre at the French Grand Prix at Longchamps. She was chosen by the Daily Express, with Sebastian Coe, as Sportsman and Sportswoman of the Year, was awarded an M.B.E. for her services to show jumping and to cap a victorious year, she signed a sponsorship deal with the oil company Tricentrol.

After five triumphant years partnering Tigre, in which together they gained nearly every top honour in Europe, it was with a very heavy heart that the part owner of Tigre bought it out from her and she finally ceased riding him in 1981. When he was finally driven away from her stables in Priors Marston in Warwickshire, Caroline was heartbroken. Tigre never performed thereafter as he had under Caroline's guidance.

Recovering from her loss, she concentrated all her efforts on her young horses and in addition giving her sponsors value for the money they had invested in her.

Her father said at the time that she changed from a hard worker to a workaholic in her efforts to find or bring on another Tigre.

By 1983 she had two horses who were beginning to win the bigger competitions – Trimoco Manuel and Trimoco Rubber Ball. In order not be caught again in the trap of not having young horses coming up, as was the case with Tigre, she drove her grade 'A' horses to the major events and with her younger horses it was a non-stop tour of the minor shows.

She was totally dedicated to her sport, thriving on unbelievable hours of work. Add to that the time she spent behind the wheel of her horsebox, and she was still able to call on reserves of energy to overcome any adversity.

Her last appearance was in the annual Suffolk Show at Ipswich in June 1983 and had ridden Trimoco Rubber Ball into second place in the first round of the jumping competition. After dismounting in the collecting ring she complained of feeling unwell and collapsed on the ground. Volunteers from the St. John's Ambulance were in attendance very soon afterwards and they did all that was humanly possible. An ambulance rushed her to Ipswich Hospital some two miles away but she was pronounced dead on arrival.

Without doubt, she had been the most outstanding and successful woman show jumper the world has ever seen.

Dorian Williams, who gave the address at Caroline's funeral in St Leonard's Church, Priors Marston, perhaps best summed up the memory of Caroline by saying: "In less than twenty years Caroline has brought more happiness and more pleasure to more people than most of us will ever do in a life time... ...the shock of Caroline's death will pass and the sadness will pass leaving us with a great pride and a great gratitude for all the pleasure and happiness and inspiration that Caroline, in her short life, gave to many thousands of people".

CAROLINE CHISHOLM

(1808–1877)

The emigrants' friend

PHILANTHROPIST Caroline Chisholm was the first person to recognise the specific human problems of emigrants, mainly young women and families who sailed on those mammoth journeys from Britain to Australia in the 19th century, and set about doing something about them. She campaigned ceaselessly to make their journeys tolerable and, when they eventually got to their destination, helped in many ways to settle them safely and in healthy conditions as well as creating opportunities to get them into employment. She also took on the British Government, lobbying to secure an acceptable and fair emigration policy.

Caroline was born 30 May 1808, almost certainly in Northampton, daughter of William and Sarah Jones. Caroline's father was a pig dealer in the town. She was the youngest of the family of twelve, at her birth her father was in his sixties and her mother much younger at thirty-seven. Due to the success of his business, William was able to provide well for his family and Caroline, like her brothers and sisters before her, received a good education including music, literature and French in which she became fluent.

In 1828 when Caroline was twenty she was introduced to Lieutenant Archibald Chisholm, an officer in the army, at a ball in

Courtesy: Northamptonshire Libraries and Information Service.

Northampton. He had spent many years abroad in the army and was serving in India where he had suffered illness and was back in England to regain his health and was stationed at Weedon Barracks.

He talked about wider world issues rather than local topics, which Caroline found exhilarating, and she found she was wanting to be a part of it. He read Greek and Latin and was fluent in Gaelic. He was also a Roman Catholic. She asked him if he would teach her Greek, and with the permission of her mother, he called at the family house on a regular basis.

He was made most welcome by all of Caroline's family and the two of them became very fond of each other. One day he proposed to her, but she would not give him an answer immediately. She had made up her mind that she wanted to be something more than an army officer's wife, something more than a partnership, and she wanted freedom to do things that she wanted to do. She told him to wait a month and if he accepted her terms, she would be willing to marry him. After the allotted time, he came back to her and they agreed to marry, in what turned out to be a long and happy partnership.

The marriage took place at the Church of the Holy Sepulchre, Northampton on 27 December 1830 and afterwards they travelled to Brighton to live while they waited for a boat to take them to India.

It was at this time that Caroline converted to Catholicism and was immersed in her new faith when Archibald, who had secured an extension to his leave until the end of 1831, sailed alone to India on 6 January 1832 to rejoin his unit. There followed a lonely period for Caroline who had to wait until 1833 to board a boat to India and eventually arrived at Madras in August when she joined her husband in an emotional reunion. At the same time she was also trying to find a new motivation in her life.

She quickly settled within the British community busying herself running the new family home. It didn't take her long to realise that officer's wives had very little to do – their servants carrying out almost all of the work and she, as a newcomer, was expected to know her place in the colony and learn how to conduct herself by observation.

The wives of the enlisted men, however, were a different kettle of fish. They had no official status and, along with any offspring, were expected to fend for themselves. The sons, more than likely, followed their father in the army, but daughters, on the other hand, generally ran wild, getting into various kinds of trouble.

Caroline decided she must do something for these unfortunate girls. She suggested the setting up of a small school for them and within a few months her idea had gained the approval of the authorities and came into being. Subjects taught in the new school were arithmetic, writing, needlework and domestic matters. A matron and teacher were recruited and, under the overall charge of Caroline, the pupils learned skills to help them lead a normal and respectable life

Caroline's first baby was a son, born 4 May 1836, and named Archibald after his father who had at that time been promoted to captain. The following year she had another son born on 5 September and named William after her father.

It was at this time that Archibald's health was once more a cause for concern and in January 1838 he was given two years secondment leave. Instead of returning home to England they decided to spend the leave in New South Wales.

The school that Caroline had founded expanded and developed and was successful for quite some time after their departure. Officially it became known as 'The Female School of Industry for the Daughters of European Soldiers'.

The Chisholm's new home was in Sydney and they quickly settled in, finding no difficulties practising Catholicism, as it was accepted within their community that they belonged to that faith.

It was not long, however, before Caroline became aware of the plight of young women who came out from Britain hoping to find a better life in Australia. On arrival they soon found out that there were no facilities to help find employment or transport to ferry them out into the bush areas to look for work. If they had little or no money, which was usually the case, they would have no roof over their heads and could be exploited and drift into prostitution. Some who found themselves pregnant would be forced to live rough facing a future of hunger and misery.

Any thought of immediate help for these unfortunate girls had to wait, however, as Caroline was expecting a third child which turned out to be another boy whom they named Henry.

Whilst walking round the port area one day with the family they came across a group of girls sitting together in the harbour looking very miserable and dirty. Caroline went over to them to ask what was the matter. It transpired they were new arrivals from Britain, they had no money and nowhere to go.

Captains of the ships who brought out the settlers got extra money by bringing out more emigrants and there was extra pressure in Britain to bring out more single females.

When they arrived at their destination they found there was no employment office and no accommodation facilities. These unfortunates had to endure horrendous journeys in cramped and unsavoury conditions and now when they were far from their homes they were defenceless and often in danger. In the end, Caroline took some of the most needy into her own home in a bid to protect them and get them settled.

Some of the settlers who had been there for a long time were horrified when they found out what she had done, telling her those girls would steal and cheat and make her life a misery, but she managed to prove them all wrong. The girls, after they had washed themselves and wore clean clothes and had a roof over their heads, turned out to be very grateful.

After enquiring amongst her friends, she found that there was indeed a need for good workers with local families. Very soon those same girls left the Chisholm household making their way to new domestic posts where they would do such jobs as cooking, cleaning and laundry work.

Later Caroline was very pleased to learn that the girls had all settled into their new jobs satisfactorily. Caroline had started a movement whereby local families began to seek domestic labour from this new market gradually eliminating the problem of the new girl settlers.

Caroline became the person to see when a settled family needed a servant girl. She would often be stopped in the street or answer a call at her house enquiring if she was the person who helped in finding employment.

Time passed and Archibald's leave was nearly over. The two decided between them that he should return to India alone leaving Caroline and the boys in Australia, allowing her to carry on her vital work whilst he served the rest of his time in the army. On his eventual return they also decided that they might go back to England to visit her family so they could see Caroline and Archibald's children for the first time.

After a tearful farewell, Caroline carried on bringing up her young family as well as helping, as best she could, the plight of the newly-arrived emigrant girls.

She had her eye on the Old Immigration Barracks in the centre of Sydney, which would make an ideal reception facility for the girls. It had been empty for some time and was infested with rats but she knew she could make it work. She met the Governor of the Colony where she made her plea but, although they parted on very good terms, he refused her request. Not to be outdone, she organised a committee of influential ladies who lobbied for the Barracks to be handed over to them so they could put it to good use. Eventually the Governor relented and Caroline and her ladies got their hands on the building.

When the rat problem had been cleared up and some decoration applied to a few of the rooms, it was ready for use. It was not ideal accommodation but it was a world away from the street life. Caroline set up a jobs register and as more girls arrived further rooms in the building were made habitable.

To supervise the domestic side of things she employed a matron, but Caroline found that to run the home properly, she would have to be there personally at night to look after the security. This meant that her three sons would have to be sent to a friend in the suburbs. It was an arrangement she disliked intensely but felt she had to make the sacrifice for the sake of her girls, some of whom were as young as thirteen (at that time the leaving age from school was twelve).

Her long-term aim was not just to get jobs for the girls in and around Sydney, she was looking for opportunities offered in the great interior. Families who had settled there were founding new communities and they needed domestic help and the single or widowed farmers needed wives.

News of Caroline's employment agency for women and girls soon spread which resulted in new people coming to see her from the outlying districts. The colony's newspaper further helped her cause by encouraging readers to send in any information about vacancies and to back the work being done to help the girls with employment in the outback.

The press also suggested that companies, who had wagons going to Sydney from the outback with supplies and were likely to return empty or partially laden, would like to give assistance to Mrs Chisholm's girls. The plea did not fall on deaf ears, offers came in to carry the girls from Sydney to the place of their future employment!

Caroline decided to travel on one of these early wagon trips to see for herself what the conditions of life were like outside of Sydney. She left the Home in trustworthy hands and travelled with a group of girls enjoying the rural scenery on their way to a new life. At the end of a day's tiring journey, they enjoyed an evening round the campfire and then, amid the sounds of the night, they fell asleep.

One by one, the settler's homesteads where jobs were waiting, were visited and at each the family came out to greet them and quickly water would be drawn and boiled for tea.

It soon became known that Mrs Chisholm's wagons brought new females into the district and resulted in great excitement. There was a new routine in the social life of the settlers with parties or other gatherings and maybe, eventually, a wedding or two.

Back in Sydney Caroline carried on her work on behalf of the new girl settlers, but she yearned to do more. She wanted to inform the powers-that-be back in England, of the conditions that these girls had to endure during their long trip from England and also what awaited them when they arrived in Australia.

She prepared a detailed questionnaire and sent a copy to as many people in as many places as she could throughout the colony. The information required covered such topics as the lifestyle of the settlers, what job opportunities were available, farming methods and yields, incomes and types of housing. Armed with this information she would be able to inform the Government in Britain of the massive potential that Australia had to offer. She would also be able to point out the vital need to reorganise and carry out a secure, fair, safe and healthy emigration policy.

Caroline's employment exchange was open every day to deal with prospective employers in person as well as a regular enquiry service by post. She was also becoming renowned for being an unofficial marriage bureau. The girls, once they were in regular employment, usually married and Caroline often received a visit from a recent newly-wed or, perhaps, was sent a piece of wedding cake. When the Home eventually closed, Caroline's expert record keeping showed she had received fifty-one pieces of wedding cake!

In 1842 Caroline wrote a book entitled *Female Immigration Considered, in a Brief Account of the Sydney Immigrants' Home* which described the difficulties of its early beginnings and the heart-rending stories of many of the girls that came to her. The book sold well and carved for itself a place in history, being the first to be published in Australia by a lady author.

With the permission of the Governor of the Colony, Caroline sent a copy of the extensive questionnaire she had compiled, to the Colonial Office in London. Some six months later came a reply thanking Mrs Chisholm for her survey and her good work on behalf of the Emigrants of New South Wales, but no further expenditure, other than what was already in place, was to be forthcoming.

In March 1845 Archibald arrived back in Sydney from India having retired from the army on health grounds before the end of his term. His return must have been a very emotional occasion allowing them, once again, to lead a complete family life after an interminable separation.

There was talk of the trip to England to see their families, but Caroline had other pressing business with which the authorities in London must be acquainted before any travel arrangements were finalised. There were ex-convicts who resolutely wanted to contact their wives and children and bring them to Australia. There were also families who had been separated and wanted reuniting. Most important was the very real need to eradicate everything that was connected with the old transportation policy.

Just before the family left for England, Caroline was publicly acknowledged for her work in the community and a gift of £150 was presented to her, which had been raised from public subscription. It was followed by heart-warming praise in the press.

The journey home was much longer than had been anticipated and, as Caroline was pregnant with their fourth child, gave birth on the ship to another boy who was given the name Sydney after their hometown in Australia.

They arrived in London in the summer of 1846. Later there was a joyous reunion with her family when she visited her hometown of Northampton. They set up home, however, in the East End of London and Caroline almost immediately started writing letters to the Colonial Land and Emigration Commissioners. She hoped she would succeed in three tasks, to obtain free transport for the convicts' wives who wished to join their husbands, to trace the children that had been separated from their families and who had sailed to Australia without them, and to assure there was proper supervision and protection of the young women going to Australia.

In 1847 the Home Office sanctioned a complimentary passage to the families of free men to travel on the female convict ship *Asia* – Caroline had achieved her first aim. Before she had heard of the Home Office announcement, Caroline was tracing the 'bounty' children who had been split from their parents. Most, it turned out, were in Ireland but only about half of the original total were to take the journey on the *Sir Edward Perry* to Australia. A doctor had been appointed to look after the children's health, along with a matron who supervised all other matters. The ship sailed from Plymouth in September 1847 not only with children, but also the families of ex-convicts who had been found too late for the journey on the *Asia*, or who were male family members and would not have been allowed to travel on the all-female ship.

In that same year Caroline had two booklets published: *Comfort for the Poor! Meat Three Times a Day* containing the human stories that she had collected during her time in Sydney, and *Emigration and Transportation* covering the moral issues – dignity, fairness and justice for the ordinary people. It was illustrated by the testimonies of settlers and a plea by Caroline for a real change of policy.

Both publications became very popular and as a result, they changed the public's assumptions that the colony was a remote territory in the back-of-beyond into a hard-working country of intense British loyalty. Caroline soon became nearly as famous in London as she was in Australia.

In June 1847 she was summoned to give evidence to a House of Lords Committee dealing with colonisation from Ireland. Here she revelled in telling the members about the opportunities offered by Australia, about the fertile land and excellent crop yields, and also took the opportunity to repeat her pleas to have the Government endorse a proper emigration policy. From that appearance before the committee, she became known as 'The Emigrants' Friend'.

In 1848 Caroline was again pregnant and in May a daughter Caroline Monica was born. With an increase in family size, a new, more suitable house was needed which they found in Charlton Crescent, Islington. There was a Catholic Church nearby, which probably led them to choose this particular house.

Caroline's next plan was to establish an emigration society, which would be an alternative to the restrictive Government scheme. In her society, an emigrating family would declare what they could pay towards the cost of their journey – the shortfall being made up in the form of loans from the society. These would be paid back once the families had settled and were financially viable.

The society was formed, being known as the Family Colonisation Loan Society ('Loan' was later dropped). Amongst the members of the committee was Northampton MP Vernon Smith. He reported that Northampton was beginning to take pride in its campaigning daughter whose determination in working for the values and responsibilities of hard-working families, was going down well in her hometown.

In late 1849 Caroline was once again pregnant and in January 1850 another daughter, Sara Monica was born, but the family joy was to be short-lived as Sara died aged six months, possibly from diphtheria.

To get over her loss, Caroline threw herself into work for the society. A ship was chartered and completely refitted to the society's standards, eradicating overcrowding and filthy conditions. The ship, *Slains Castle*, was due to sail in late September 1850, the first journey under the auspices of the society, and in celebration of this, a large meeting and rally was organised and Caroline was cheered as she rose to address the audience. She told them that it was the first ship where families had travelled together along with single women. At the end of her speech she was given three cheers.

The *Slains Castle* sailed from London to its first stop at Gravesend. On that short leg Caroline was onboard making tours of the ship to see all was well. After the Sunday morning religious services for various denominations were over, Caroline made her way onshore and saw her first group of settlers off to a new life in Australia.

Some time later it became clear that the society would need someone in Sydney to administer business at that end and manage the repayment of loans. No one had been found in Sydney and so eventually, after much discussion, Archibald was to be the one. This meant another lengthy separation, all the more heart-rending, as Caroline was expecting another child.

Archibald sailed in March 1851, the baby, Harriet Monica, was born in July at about the same time as Archibald arrived in Australia.

Caroline, in the meantime, carried on lobbying for proper family emigration and was invited to speak in many towns all over England and Ireland. She was also influential in the Royal Ascent of the Passenger Amendment Act 1852 in which the Government ordered that minimum standards for passengers must be met. Caroline now saw that the British Government was beginning to take notice of her advice as well as the views and aspirations of the settlers in Australia.

With Archibald manning the Sydney end of the society, its emigrant ships were now leaving the home country in large numbers. Caroline's reputation struck a note with one ship owner – W S Lindsay – who was also a long-time shipping reformer. He built a ship in her honour, constructing the internal features based on Caroline's instructions, which would act as a model for other emigrant ships and then named her *Caroline Chisholm*.

After more than three years of separation from her husband, Caroline made preparations to travel back to Australia with her family to rejoin Archibald. It had been planned to return on the ship bearing her name but that had been requisitioned by the Government for war duty in the Crimea and so she eventually sailed in the *Ballarat*, which finally docked in Melbourne in July 1854. A large crowd was there to greet her and loud cheering was heard when she appeared on deck, but the real welcome was seeing Archibald again, once more reuniting her family.

During the next few years Caroline continued to work tirelessly on behalf of others. The family stayed in Melbourne for a time and then moved to Kyneton when she established a series of ten no-frills, but relatively strong, buildings at various places alongside main highways for the use of people making very long journeys. The buildings, called 'Shelter Sheds' or 'Protection Posts' were provided with water and wood fuel and the cost per night was one shilling (5p) for an adult and sixpence ($2^{1}/2$ p) for a child.

After twelve years living in Australia, a family decision was made to return to England and retirement. Neither Caroline nor Archibald was in good health.

On returning to England they settled in Liverpool and although they lived quietly, Caroline was not forgotten for she was awarded a Government pension of £100 per annum for her past service. She suffered periods of illness in the 1860s and 70s and spent the last years of her life in London. She had never shaken off a kidney disease she contracted in Australia and during an attack of bronchitis she died 25 March 1877 aged 69.

It had been decided that she be buried in Northampton. Her body was brought to the town and rested overnight in the south aisle of the Roman Catholic Cathedral. The next day interment took place just after mid-day at the Billing Road Cemetery, the chief mourners being Miss Chisholm and Mr Gray. Archibald did not attend, as he was seriously ill in London. The crowd, who came to pay their last respects, filed past the grave and many tossed in posies of spring flowers.

Caroline slipped into obscurity in Australia for about three quarters of a century but interest in her surfaced again in 1949 when an electoral ward consisting of the eastern suburbs of Melbourne was named after her. In 1960 the Australian Government depicted her portrait on the five-dollar banknote to commemorate her outstanding service to the underprivileged of Australia. In the 1992 edition, however, her portrait had been removed and replaced by Queen Elizabeth II. A Caroline Chisholm stamp was issued in 1968 and in 1994 she was posthumously awarded the Medal of the Order of Australia. There is Caroline Chisholm Catholic College at Regentville, a Caroline Chisholm Library and in the LaTrobe University in Melbourne a Caroline Chisholm Hall where the annual Lecture in her name is delivered.

What of Northampton? It has taken 127 years for the town of her birth to recognise her national and international achievements. A new school at Wootton Fields, has been named after her and is sited in a most appropriate place – her father was born in nearby Wootton.

For years her grave had been left to the ravages of time until 1977 (the centenary of her death) when questions were asked in the State Parliament at Melbourne regarding the condition of it. Since that time it has been maintained by various people and organisations.

COURTNEY HOPE

(1886–1975)

Widow Turvey

A WOMAN OF MANY ROLES, Courtney was involved with public and community service, writing, sport, and the entertainment business. In the latter role, she commenced in amateur productions, stepping up a gear in middle age to the professional world of radio and films. She kept the family name of Hope for her stage name but admitted she did not really know how Courtney came about.

Dorothy Sybil Hope was born on 19 December 1886 in Wellingborough, the daughter of William and Bertha. Her father was a dental surgeon and the family home was 'Hopedene', Hatton Park, in the town. William Hope was for many years a well-known amateur performer and it was with him, in 1896, when she was a schoolgirl,

Dorothy first appeared on stage in a farce at the old Corn Exchange in Wellingborough. The name of the play has been forgotten, but it showed, from that early age, she had already developed a love for the stage.

Her mother was a keen devotee to hunting, an amateur photographer, a golfer and, in later years, turned her hand to croquet. She became very successful in the sport becoming English champion in 1919, whilst two years later, as an international player, won the French Gold Cup.

Dorothy first met the man who was to

become her husband, when she was about eight years old. They were both members of the congregation of All Hallows' Church, Wellingborough. She was so smitten by him, that she wrote in her Prayer Book: "Please God let me marry that boy" and indeed that is what happened, but it was to be some years later that they met socially in a dramatic society.

Her husband, whom she married in 1908, was well-known Wellingborough solicitor Sidney H S Cook and they were to have two daughters, one of whom followed her mother in a career on the stage.

In that same year when they married, the couple and others, became founder members of Wellingborough Amateur Operatic Society. For years afterwards they both took part in the productions.

Dorothy also founded the Hatton Dramatic Company and from it sprang *Mrs Cook's Concert Party*, a show organised by Dorothy herself in which for a long time she wrote the sketches and monologues as well as taking the rehearsals. The concert party ran for a number of years leading up to the Second World War, touring towns and villages in the winter months within a thirty-mile radius of Wellingborough. It was all in aid of charity and raised much needed cash for hospitals, church funds and other worthy causes.

Some of her monologues and sketches have been published in five titles including *Fun for the Footlights*, *More Footlight Fun* and *Footlight Fun Encore*. They are very popular with various organisations, especially in the English-speaking countries of the Commonwealth. Even though some are now a bit dated, particularly where they mention ration books and coupons and long queues in the shops reminiscent of the time during the Second World War, people still like to perform them.

It was to be one of these monologues that eventually led her to work for BBC radio. Martyn C Webster, a BBC producer, came to Northampton to conduct auditions in the town in the mid 1930s in order to discover talent he could use in the medium of radio. A friend of Dorothy's bet her five shillings (25 pence) that she dare not go, she took on the challenge and made her way, with others from her concert party, to Fraser Son & McKenzie's music shop in Fish Street where she recited a monologue and managed to make Mr Webster chuckle.

Having heard nothing from the BBC for a whole year, she decided to take the bull by the horns and wrote to the producer asking him if he remembered laughing at her offering, one wet Monday morning twelve months previously in Northampton. In his reply he said he did remember and invited her to take a selection of her material to the studio in Birmingham. After that second audition she managed to acquire a BBC contract on her terms, which turned out to provide her with radio work for virtually the rest of her life.

Her contract led to parts in such programmes as the first Paul Temple series, *Appointment with Fear* with Valentine Dyall and housekeeper Betsy Horrocks in the daily fifteen-minute serial *Dick Barton Special Agent*. She was also the first Mrs Freeman in *Mrs Dale's Diary*. Other appearances included *Just William*, *Guilty Party*, *Radio Ruffles*, as well as countless parts in *Saturday Night Theatre*.

In her experience of early radio, she said the actors made all the sound effects themselves, but later on, except for things like opening a letter or drinking from a glass or cup, these were done from recordings. If there was a drowning at sea, the actors never heard the wind and the waves, only the showing of coloured lights to indicate that the sounds were being added to the programme.

In 1949, at the age of 63, she achieved a long-standing ambition, by being offered a part in a feature film called *Meet Simon Cherry* ('the Rev'). It was a thriller based on a successful radio series *Meet the Rev*, shot at the Cookham Film Studios and took five weeks to complete.

A few weeks later she started work on her second film called *The Man in Black*, starring Sid James and Valentine Dyall. It was another thriller, also based on the popular radio series *Appointment with Fear*, with Dorothy taking the part of a housekeeper. She also appeared in two more films in 1952, *The Last Page* and *Wings of Danger*.

She is, perhaps, best remembered for playing Widow Turvey in *The Archers*, a part she was offered in September 1954 and continued to play on a regular basis until a few weeks before her death in 1975. At the time she was believed to be the oldest person on the BBC's payroll. The thing she remembered most about being in *The Archers* was how she and poor Walter Gabriel, when they were both featured together, used to argue their way through the scripts.

Apart from her work on radio and in films, she was also prominent in the life of Wellingborough. In 1936 she was appointed a magistrate – being only the fourth woman to hold that position in the town. When she was obliged to retire on reaching the age of 75, she told a reporter, "... I was considered too old for working on the Bench," and then added, "Too old, indeed!"

During the Second World War she was the Women's Royal Voluntary Service centre organiser at their office in Oxford Street, Wellingborough.

One of the WRVS personnel remembered Dorothy trudging down to the office five days a week, inspiring all the ladies to do their bit for the war effort.

In 1959 she was elected president of the Wellingborough Amateur Operatic Society, a post she held until she resigned at the age of 81.

Sport was another of her keen interests. In 1954, at the inception of Wellingborough Bowling Club, Women's Section, she was elected President. In golf she was captain of Wellingborough Ladies' Club, and was, for a time, a member of the committee organising lawn tennis tournaments in the town.

She was president of the Northamptonshire branch of the NSPCC as well as secretary of the Wellingborough branch, also a member and past president of the Women's Section of Wellingborough British Legion.

If that was not enough, as a practising Christian, she was a dedicated worker for all of her life at All Hallows' Church in Wellingborough.

For many years she lived alone (her husband died in 1945) in the house where he was born – Priory Cottage in Church Street, next to All Hallows, but following a short period of illness in 1973, she decided to move to Burrough-on-the-Hill in Leicestershire, to live with her married daughter. It was there that she died on 17 January 1975.

At her funeral, All Hallows' Church was filled to capacity with family and friends, town dignitaries, radio personalities and members of the public who had gathered to pay their last respects to a loved Wellingburian. Among the cast of *The Archers* present were Norman Painting (Phil Archer), Anne Cullen (Carol Tregorran) and Molly Harris (Martha Woodford).

Tony Shryane, producer of *The Archers* said: "Although she was 88 when she last came to the studio to record several weeks ago, she amazed all of us with her vitality and good humour."

She was once asked, after giving one of her many talks, if there was one thing she would liked to have done and had not yet accomplished. She replied: "Yes, act, I would like to have been another Edith Evans."

She never forgot the man who helped her with her professional career. In her will, she left Martyn C Webster of the BBC, her Chinese lacquer table with matching mirror as a token of her gratitude to him for giving her the opportunity of working for the British Broadcasting Corporation.

ELIZABETH JEAN HARWOOD

(1938–1990)

Supremo soprano

O N 27 May 1938, in Barton Seagrave, a baby girl was born who was destined to become a world famous soprano. Elizabeth Harwood, the survivor of twins, was the daughter of Sidney Curtis Harwood and his wife Constance.

Sidney, who was from Scarborough, came to the county to take up

the post of Deputy Clerk to the old Kettering Urban Council and chose to live in the village of Rushton.

Constance Read, his future wife, was one of four children of a Rothwell carpenter, builder and farmer. Her father was a local preacher and his children were brought up in the 'full-throated tradition of singing, beloved of the Free Churches'. After taking singing tuition from the Rev Greville Cooke, Rector of Cransley, Constance became well-known to local

Courtesy: Elizabeth Harwood Memorial Trust.

audiences performing regularly in concert and operatic society events. She eventually turned professional and at the apogee of her career took part in a broadcast from Southwark Cathedral.

Sidney was also musical, being a fine tenor, and was often in demand for concerts in the district. The couple met in Rothwell Methodist Church where they both attended and eventually married making their home in Warkton Lane, Barton Seagrave. There they regularly rehearsed their repertoire with such gusto, which eventually led to complaints from the neighbours. They overcame this hurdle by selling their house and moving, but only to the other side of the road, where their new neighbours were more amenable.

In the same year that Elizabeth was born, the family left Barton Seagrave and moved to Yorkshire where Sidney secured the position of Clerk to Skipton Rural Council.

Constance taught Elizabeth singing from her early years until the teenager was accepted for a place at the Royal Manchester College of Music, where she attended between the years of 1955 and 1960. An experience Elizabeth often referred to as being some of the happiest days of her life.

As she was showing great potential in her studies, the Principal of the College encouraged Elizabeth towards opera because of her good looks and her glowing and bubbly personality, which he said were ideal for the stage.

In her final year, at the age of 22, she won the Kathleen Ferrier Memorial Prize, which amounted to £300 and was presented to her at a ceremony in The Wigmore Hall in London. The prize money enabled her to travel to Italy for a year to study under Lina Pagliughi. Whilst there she entered the Verdi Competition in Busseto and was delighted to become joint winner.

After graduating, her first professional contract was in 1960 as Second Boy in the *Magic Flute* at Glyndebourne, Sussex. In 1961 she joined Sadlers Wells Opera soon becoming the first-choice soprano in operas such as *The Abduction from the Harem* (Constanza), *Count Ory* (Countess Adele) and *Rigoletto* (Gilda). Here she worked under Colin Davis, the artistic director, who was an early influence on Elizabeth's professional career.

During the five years she was at Sadlers Wells, she was able to learn her repertoire and, using that experience, she joined the Sutherland Williamson Grand Opera Company in 1965 in order to launch her international career. A tour of Australia followed with Elizabeth alternating with Joan Sutherland in the leading roles. She also appeared with Luciano Pavarotti in *Lucia di Lammermore*, *Elixir of Love* and *La Sonnambula*.

In 1966 Elizabeth married businessman Julian A C Royle and they had one son Nicholas.

The following year she joined The English Opera Group to sing Galatea in *Handel's Acis* and Galatea in performances at the Aldeburgh Festival, Drottnigholm in Sweden and Versailles in France. She made such an impression in France that she was invited to perform Donna Elvira in *Don Giovanni* at the Aix-en-Provence Festival. That same year, 1967, she made her debut at Covent Garden, London, in *Arabella*, singing the role of Fiakermilli.

Her performance at the Aix-en-Provence Festival attracted the attention of none other than Herbert von Karajan, the world-famous conductor. He was so taken with Elizabeth's performance, he invited her to take the parts of Constanza in *Die Entfurhrung* and Fiordigili in *Cosi Fan Tutte* in the 1969 Saltzburg Festival.

In the following year she returned to Saltzburg to perform the role of the Countess in *The Marriage of Figaro* which was produced and directed by von Karajan.

Elizabeth's favourite composer was, without doubt, Mozart, and she was to perform his works in major productions at such places as La Scala, Milan (*The Abduction from the Harem* and *Benvenuto Cellini*), Metropolitan Opera, New York (*Cosi Fan Tutte* and *Don Giovanni*), Covent Garden, (*Rigoletto*, *Don Pasquale*, *Arabella*, *The Masked Ball* among others) and Glyndebourne (*The Magic Flute*, *Cosi Fan Tutte*, *The Marriage of Figaro* and *Der Rosenkavalier*).

Her last operatic performance was in *La Colombe* for the Buxton Festival and performed at Sadlers Wells in 1983.

In the 1980s she devoted more of her time to the concert and recital aspect of her profession and she was likely to be found at the Wigmore Hall or Queen Elizabeth Hall rather than at Covent Garden. She very much enjoyed singing oratorios, performing in *Messiah* over 100 times – the first being when she stepped in for her mother when Constance was indisposed.

In the same decade she had successful tours to New Zealand, Australia and British Colombia. Closer to home, she delighted the French population by her rapport with pianist Moura Lympany and the Manchester Camerata at the Rasigueres Festival of Wine and Music.

Elizabeth was very committed to her Master Classes where she encouraged young singers to excel in their chosen careers. She also found great satisfaction from musical evenings at her home in Essex.

After dinner she would sit at the piano and encourage some of those present to join her in singing pieces from her repertoire.

In her will, made in 1982, she left instructions for a prize to be established in the gift of her mother, which is now incorporated in The Elizabeth Harwood Memorial Trust. It provides a 'Scholarship to enable a singer from the Royal Northern College of Music who is judged by the Adjudicators to have the greatest promise for an operatic career, with special reference to the works of Mozart, to pursue further specialised studies'. It has been presented annually since 1992.

Although she expressed total loyalty to Yorkshire, she did return to her native Northamptonshire to sing at various times. There was a Festival at Desborough, a concert in the parish church at Rothwell and a charity event at Boughton House, the Northamptonshire home of the Duke of Buccleugh.

After a busy season or a prolonged tour Elizabeth loved nothing more than to relax in the family home in rural Essex with her husband and son as well as her cats, Spiro the poodle and Bluebell, the family donkey.

She died 22 June 1990 aged 52. Dame Janet Baker paying tribute to her said: "...she was the most beloved of my colleagues, a beautiful person in every way. Her art lit up the stage..."

A service of celebration and thanksgiving for the life of Elizabeth was held at St Paul's Church, Covent Garden, in October 1990.

A selection of dresses Elizabeth wore on stage is on show in the museum of Renishaw Hall in Derbyshire, the ancestral home of the Sitwell family.

A plaque to her memory is in St Mary the Virgin Church, Fryerning, Essex.

ELIZABETH WOODVILLE

(*c.*1437–1492)

A queen beneath an oak tree

A FUTURE Queen of England, Elizabeth Woodville was almost certainly born at Grafton Regis about 1437. She married first to Sir John Grey of Groby in Leicestershire, but he was killed at the Second Battle of St Albans in 1461. His estates were confiscated by Edward IV and Elizabeth returned to Grafton Regis.

Four years later, Edward came to Northamptonshire to hunt in Whittlewood Forest. Hearing he was in the district, Elizabeth sought him in the forest to personally plead for the return of her late husband's lands. They met, as tradition has it, under an oak tree, known ever since as 'The Queen's Oak'.

Edward was struck by Elizabeth's beauty, immediately falling in love with her. They were married secretly in a ceremony at Grafton Regis on 1 May 1464.

Courtesy: Northamptonshire Libraries and Information Service.

54

The King did not divulge his union to his ministers until September 1464 when he publicly avowed his marriage and Elizabeth was declared Queen and crowned in Westminster on 20 May 1465.

From spending her earliest years in relative obscurity, she was to become sister-in-law of Richard III, mother-in-law of Henry VII, grandmother of Henry VIII and mother of Edward V.

Edward IV and Elizabeth had ten children; seven daughters and three sons, two of whom were Edward and Richard (the Princes in the Tower). The other son George died young.

Edward IV died 9 April 1483 and plans were made for a quick coronation of their son Edward V, but the Duke of Gloucester (later Richard III) captured the young king and imprisoned him in the Tower of London.

Elizabeth withdrew to sanctuary at Westminster with her other son Richard but later agreed to hand him over to the Duke of Gloucester so that the young prince could be with his brother.

In 1484 Elizabeth left sanctuary and submitted to Richard III (who had usurped the Crown) and he granted her an allowance to live on. Three years later she returned to sanctuary at Bermondsey Abbey where she died on 8 June 1492 and was buried, with little pomp, beside her husband in St George's Chapel, Windsor on 12 June.

In 1465, Elizabeth refounded and endowed Queens' College, Cambridge.

MARY L PENDERED

(1858–1940)

Writer, novelist and playwright

O NE OF NORTHAMPTONSHIRE'S most versatile and prolific authors, Mary Lucy Pendered was born in Camberwell, Surrey in 1858, the daughter of Thomas Pendered who was the founder of the well-known Wellingborough firm of auctioneers. Pendered's are still operating in the town as estate agents. Her grandfather was an organ builder and it was probably from this ancestor that she acquired her talent for music, alongside her literary aptitude.

She came to live in Wellingborough at the age of seven in 1864, the family home being in Cambridge Street. Her formative years in Wellingborough were described years later in a series of articles she called *Memories of Wellingborough*, which appeared in the Wellingborough News.

Her literary career began whilst she was still living at home when she began to write short stories. Her first major success was a serial based on *Sins of the Fathers* by Mark Melford, which was accepted for

publication and appeared in a Yorkshire newspaper.

In 1892 she left home, to the annoyance of her parents, in order to work in a newspaper office in London. The publication concerned was a society weekly called Life for which she received a wage of £1 per

Courtesy: Northamptonshire Libraries and Information Service.

56

week, a job she later described as doing 'everything except sweep out the office'. Later she managed to get onto the staff of the London edition of the Detroit Free Press as a sub editor.

Later still she spent some months in Scotland reporting for the Oban Times. At the same time she also wrote book reviews for the London Daily Chronicle.

During her time in London she met a number of literary celebrities including George Bernard Shaw and Hall Cain who left lasting impressions on her, so much so, she joined the Fabian Society and was to hold Socialist principles for the rest of her life.

Her first novel, published in 1893, was *Dust and Laurels* which sold in excess of 3000 copies. Two years later *A Pastoral Play Out* appeared and was even more successful but this too was outshone in 1899 by her next offering entitled *An Englishman*, which a leading literary critic of the time, thought it one of the best six novels of the year.

Much speculation occurred when she published anonymously in 1905 *The Truth About Men* (by a spinster). It was written as a reply to Thomas W H Crosland's book (1903) *Lovely Woman* in which the author insulted the female gender. The Yorkshire Post lambasted the unknown author, guessing her to be a woman and calling her a minx. On the other hand, the book critic in The Evening Standard enquired: "Who is this spinster? She has written a remarkably clever book." Moreover, The Sunday Times referred to it as 'this audacious and really clever brochure', which went on to sell over 7000 copies.

The Fair Quaker published in 1910 is an historical account of Hannah Lightfoot, the beautiful Quaker girl, said by scandal to have secretly married George III when he was Prince of Wales – a subject of abiding interest to Mary.

She considered her best book to be *Secret Battlefield* (1918) although it turned out to be not as popular as some of her other work. It was written during the years of the First World War, but people were not keen to read it because of the title. In fact it had nothing to do with war at all.

Between the years 1903 and 1934 she wrote and had published some eighteen titles. The one, which took the least time to produce, was in 1911 and called *Daisy the Minx*. She was able to write, revise and type all within a month.

On 27 March 1933 an hour-long radio programme, written by Mary entitled *A Pageant of Northamptonshire* was broadcast by the BBC Midland Region. It portrayed the county's rich heritage from Hereward the Wake to the Restoration of the Monarchy in 1661. Amongst the historical characters included were Simon de Senlis who founded the Church of the Holy Sepulchre in Northampton, poets John Dryden, John Clare, John Askham, artist Alfred East and the Montagu family of Boughton House.

It was an enormous task to research and write and, as she wrote afterwards: "I beg all my readers to consider the task of pressing all Northamptonshire into the mould of one hour! Then I feel sure, they will make allowance for any shortcomings."

In 1939, as a confirmed pacifist, she wrote a play *The Princess, or Pretender* (in collaboration with Justinian Mallett) which was vigorously anti-war, denouncing armament manufacture and pleading for the banishment of fear between European nations leading up to the Second World War. It was given a Sunday evening performance at the Palace Theatre, Wellingborough under the auspices of the League of Nations Union, and Mary gave a curtain speech. It was also performed in many other places in the county including Kettering and Rushden.

Preferring to write sitting in a comfortable armchair with a footstool and writing board on her knee, she was always busy on a book, article, short story or perhaps writing to the press about anything which took her interest.

Her hobbies included music, gardening and public work. An example of the latter occurred in 1892 when the railwaymen in Wellingborough felt they ought to raise funds for their 'Orphan Fund'. They approached Mary, who with her usual enthusiasm arranged a successful concert with artistes from London and the county. It proved so successful, it was repeated annually for many years, resulting in large amounts of money being raised for the Orphan Fund.

Although Mary never married and had a family of her own, she encouraged young people with literary interests to strive for success; her home at 'Redwell' was often 'open house'. Among those she enthused were Reginald Underwood of Finedon and H E Bates formerly of Rushden.

After her brother died in 1934, she moved from Redwell to a house in Great Addington where she took a great deal of interest in the life of the village and was also the backbone of the Women's Institute.

In a moving tribute to Mary after her death in 1940, Reginald Underwood, author and musician of Finedon said: "she had great histrionic gifts and all those who ever saw her on a platform know, she would have made a fine actress. She had been an excellent singer and pianist. She was a capital reciter, but she often complained that versatility had been her curse, that she should have specialised."

RUBY MURRAY

(1935–1996)

The heartbeat girl

IN THE SHORT-LIVED WORLD of popular music, Ruby Murray was a star whose talents earned her a place in the *Guinness Book of Theatrical Records*. Her husky voice and girl-next-door image endeared her to millions of fans. The beginning of her career consisted of a meteoric rise to stardom when she had five record singles at one time in the Top Twenty.

Ruby Florence Campbell Murray daughter of Daniel and Winifred was born 29 March 1935 at Moltick Street, off the Donegal Road in Belfast, Northern Ireland.

At about six weeks old she had an operation on swollen glands which resulted in her having a particularly husky voice. Ruby often quipped that her mother left her out in the rain when she was young and got rusty!

At the age of four she was taken to the Belfast Empire to see, amongst others, G H Elliott's very famous act *A Chocolate Coloured Coon* – an indication as to how different the entertainment business was in those days. From then on she was determined to go on the stage herself.

Her father, known as 'Big Dan', used to put on amateur concerts in the Ulster Hall, Belfast and it was in one of these shows that she made her stage debut.

Sitting in the audience, looking for promising talent, was television producer Richard Afton. He was impressed by the performance of this twelve-year-old and gave her a contract to appear on British television at the Alexandra Palace studios where she made her professional debut. She had, however, been paid as a child performer for quite some time before being seen by Richard Afton.

Strict Irish laws concerning child performers meant she had to return to school until she was fourteen after which she had a succession of jobs including a handkerchief factory, a sweet shop and at a bakery – jobs she really didn't want – it was to be show business only for Ruby.

In 1949 she managed to get a part in a variety show which toured Northern Ireland called *Top Flight Stars* with Joseph Locke and Ronnie Carroll. As Ruby was still quite young, her mother accompanied her for the duration of the tour.

In the same year she appeared in a summer season review – *The Tommy Morgan Show* at the Glasgow Pavilion, returning to Northern Ireland to tour – in a hired lorry – a show called *Holiday Express*.

When she was sixteen she was successful in getting the singing part in a revue which toured the Republic of Ireland called *Yankee Doodle Blarney*. The tour ended in England at the Metropolitan Theatre, Edgware Road, London where once again she was watched by Richard Afton.

He was on the look out for a singer to replace Joan Regan in his BBC Television series *Quite Contrary*. Again being very impressed by her performance, he offered her the job.

During that first television show she was spotted by British record producer Ray Martin, who immediately signed her for a recording contract with E.M.I's Colombia UK label.

The first release *Get Well Soon* made little impression but following on, *Heartbeat* zoomed into the Top Twenty best selling discs at No. 3. The next record was *Softly, Softly* which shot to the top of the hit parade. It suited ideally her husky tones and shy, reserved style and became her very own signature tune for the rest of her life.

Barely twelve weeks had passed when Ruby had amassed five records simultaneously in the best-selling record charts, staying there for three months. This was a feat that has never been beaten – only equalled by Elvis Presley.

The other three successes were *Happy Days and Lonely Nights* (No. 4); *If Anyone Finds Finds This I Love You* (No. 5) and *Evermore* (No. 6).

Readers of *New Musical Express* voted her the country's favourite female vocalist, receiving a thousand more votes than Alma Cogan, her nearest rival.

As result of these successes she was signed up by Bernard Delfont's Agency and was soon packing in audiences at theatres up and down the country. In August 1955 she appeared with Norman Wisdom at the London Palladium in a show called *Painting the Town* which ran for

Courtesy: Bernie Burgess.

seven months. Ruby also appeared in the *Royal Variety Performance* for that year.

In 1956 she got the part of an Irish chambermaid in a film starring Frankie Howerd called *Touch of the Sun*. Later in the same year she was on television again singing and dancing with Tommy Steele in *The Golden Year*.

The first summer season promoted by Bernard Delfont was in 1957, Ruby topped the bill with comic and magician Tommy Cooper. It was during this show that she was to meet her future husband.

Bernard (Bernie) Burgess was born in Oxford but came to Northampton when he was 12. After leaving school he wanted to do only one job and that had to be connected with the stage. His father Leonard was an electrician at the New Theatre, Northampton and had taken Bernie, from the age of twelve, to the theatre at various times in connection with his job and this is where Bernie learnt all about provincial theatre behind the scenes.

He was heard one day singing back stage by a group called the Mell-O-Macs who asked him to join their act. Later they changed their name to The Jones Boys and, after a month's intensive rehearsals and revisions, took to the road winning many fans along the way. They toured extensively in variety and eventually topped the bill in their own right. They also appeared frequently on television as well as securing a recording contract with Decca Records.

Bernie had first met Ruby towards the end of April 1957 during rehearsals for the Blackpool show. Ruby said he tended to be on his own when he was not working, spending much time fishing off the end of the pier.

She began to look forward to meeting him after rehearsals and he took her out to supper and before very long – love took over!

Ruby and Bernie were keen to get married. Unfortunately, Ruby's parents, who were in Blackpool living in a house that Ruby had rented for the season, were hostile to Ruby's relationship with Bernie. Knowing that her parents would never agree to the marriage, they decided to tie the knot in secret and inform them afterwards.

They married at Whitegate Baptist Church in Blackpool on 23 August, just under two weeks after becoming engaged. Ruby wore a black velvet suit and is quoted afterwards as saying: "Bernie is everything I ever wanted..."

That night after the show a huge wedding cake was cut and twelve bottles of champagne for the cast was drunk. They spent a belated honeymoon in Paris at the end of the season.

Christmas was spent in separate pantomimes: Ruby in *Babes in the Wood* at Liverpool and Bernie in Birmingham.

In 1958 Ruby went to America to appear in *The Patti Page Show* and on her return went immediately into a summer show at Great Yarmouth again with Tommy Cooper and The Jones Boys.

That same year the pair bought a permanent home – a bungalow at Oxshott in Surrey – and they appeared in a number of magazine articles showing the happy couple in blissful domesticity, but the happy family image was not quite what it seemed. They were experiencing major difficulties in their marriage caused by outside influences.

1959 saw Ruby, accompanied by Bernie, return to America for a second tour. Back home again they made preparations for the journey to entertain British troops in Malta, Cyprus and Tripoli.

At this time she was expecting their first child and had decided to have the baby in Northampton because that is where they had lived at the beginning of their marriage.

They had got to know and liked very much one of the gynaecologists, Mr Watson, a highly respected Consultant at the Barratt Maternity Home. Bernie had recently left The Jones Boys and would be at home to help with the new baby.

Julie Amanda was born 5 May 1960 at the Barratt Maternity Home, she was suffering from jaundice but Ruby said after the new-born was put into her arms, "She had a mass of red hair... she was so beautiful."

Julie was christened at the church in Blackpool where her parents were married, she was six weeks old and her mother was back in a show at The Palace with Harry Secombe and Harry Worth.

With Bernie staying to help look after Amanda, the family enjoyed their time in a rented house during that summer season.

In 1963 they sold their house in Surrey and purchased Rectory Cottage in Wootton just outside Northampton, into which they moved in August of that year. It was in need of renovation due to dry rot in the flooring and both the bathroom and kitchen required complete modernisation. It was set in a third of an acre of land, allowing them room to build an extension.

Wootton was an ideal location for the family. Bernie was close to his adopted hometown and family and Ruby found it useful to be in the centre of the country adjacent to the M1 motorway, providing an ideal base from which to travel to her engagements.

After a troops tour of Aden and the Persian Gulf, it was another summer season at Great Yarmouth (this time without Bernie) and then home to Wootton to await the birth of their second child.

Timothy John was born 3 February 1965, again at the Barratt Maternity Home. The proud parents were relieved at the successful birth but were apprehensive when Tim was more jaundiced than his sister.

Ruby was in Canada in 1969 for an appearance in a British style television show, similar to *Stars and Garters*. It was a family occasion when Bernie and the children accompanied her.

Their marriage was under strain due to unrelenting outside pressure but both put in extra work to try to make a go of it.

In 1971 she was in Paignton, Devon in a show at the Festival Hall with comedian Max Wall. During that season she renewed the acquaintance of an old friend Ray Lamar whom she had not seen for years.

Ruby filed for divorce in 1974 but, after a heart to heart talk with Bernie, they agreed once more to try and make their marriage work.

The situation did not improve and Ruby suffered a nervous breakdown, and was admitted to hospital where she stayed for a month.

Within two years she suffered a relapse and was again admitted to hospital with another breakdown.

She was advised by her doctors to seriously think about leaving her home environment before she got any worse. She took their advice and decided to go to Devon to join Ray Lamar. She had been seeing him quite often and had decided to live with him.

Ruby and Bernie were divorced in 1977 and she agreed that Bernie should have custody of the children.

She married for the second time in 1993 to Ray Lamar and their home was in Torquay.

In early December 1996 she became seriously ill and was admitted to Torbay Hospital where she died 17 December. By her bedside were Bernie, who had kept vigil for five days and nights, and their children Julie and Tim.

She had been in show business for nearly 50 years and had travelled the world. When she sang one could understand every word and she had an incredibly infectious smile.

SISTER MARY WARD

(1885–1972)

Florence Nightingale of the canals

FOR NEARLY THIRTY YEARS, during the mid-twentieth century, Sister Mary Ward was the self-appointed nurse and friend of the canal boat people. For most of that period she operated from a surgery on the lock side at Stoke Bruerne. She always defended the boat families and often used to say: "They need me, I'm the only one who understands them."

Mary Hollowell Amos and twin sister Ellen were born in 1885, their birth was registered in the June quarter of that year. They were the daughters of Thomas and Sarah of Stoke Bruerne.

Thomas was a rope and twine manufacturer in the village, carrying on the business from his father and grandfather, he was also a J.P.

Mary always wanted to be a nurse from her earliest memories and said as a child she did not generally like to play with her dolls, but if they got broken heads or limbs, that was a different story – she could then 'nurse' them back to health.

Being brought up in a canal environment, she grew to love the canal boats and particularly the people who worked them. She and her twin sister also fell in love with the babies on the boats, the mothers often allowing the girls to take them to their parent's house where they could look after them.

In her younger days Sister Mary had a hip disorder resulting in one of her legs being shorter than the other. To correct the situation, her father paid for a special surgical boot to be made which was built up to allow her to walk reasonably well without too much of a limp.

As she got older she dearly wanted to train as a nurse but was refused by the medical authorities because of the condition of her leg. She was

very bitter over this decision saying she had been turned out of the country!

Not to be thwarted, her father arranged for Mary to go to Paris to train as a nurse there. She eventually spent twelve years nursing on the Continent as well as working as a surgery assistant. She worked mainly in convents, being known as Sister Mary of our Blessed Lady.

During her time there, her hip condition was successfully corrected by a French surgeon, allowing her to finally dispense with her surgical boot.

She was also involved in the nursing of chronically sick patients travelling between England and the United States of America.

She returned to Stoke Bruerne in 1934 to nurse her sick father. Having previously been used to treating hundreds of patients, she found that just treating her father was far from fulfilling.

Her father agreed and suggested that it would be nice if she would look after the boat people. Few people understood them and it would be a very rewarding job. As a child she knew all the boat families that came to the village and had got on with them so well that she decided to give it a try.

Starting off treating everyday conditions such as cuts, bruises and strains, she found that the number of patients gradually increased until she was forced to turn the morning room in the house into a proper surgery. In turn, and to be fair, she invited all those who worked on the canal to use her services.

From that time she was on call night and day treating such things as burns, stitching cuts and delivering babies. From her experience of the boat people she remembered many new born babies dying and even more died during their first year. Things gradually got better, however, until it became the exception rather than the rule.

When she first started as a midwife, she usually had no knowledge that a baby was on the way. The husband would arrive unannounced to fetch her and together off they would go to the cramped quarters of a canal boat to bring a new life into the world.

She was grateful that during her experience of midwifery, she did not have to deal with any serious complications, but openly admitted she did, on occasion, come out in a cold sweat wondering what might have occurred if things had gone wrong.

She also did other things not connected with the medical profession such as reading out mail and writing letters, including many love letters. When asked what she should write, the answer was usually: "You know better than I what to say, Sister Mary".

For the first fifteen years Sister Mary financed the surgery out of her own pocket. After that time the funds began to run out and she decided she would have to cut her losses and close it down. The Grand Union Canal Company heard of her plight and came to the rescue, giving the surgery their blessing, and paying Sister Mary a salary as well as funding the cost of the drugs she used. Her new official title was 'Consultant Sister to long-distance boatmen and families, British Canals'.

She married a Charlie Ward who eventually took over her father's rope business and also ran the rope and grocery shop when her father became too frail. Later Charlie moved the business to a vacant stonemason's shed by Lock 15, which enabled his wife to move her surgery into the old shop premises where she continued her work.

In addition to her obligations to the boat people, she also carried out tasks for the local community. At the village school she was the medical advisor and nurse, and was on hand as midwife when called upon for families in the surrounding area.

At Christmas time she would dress up as Father Christmas and deliver presents to any boat families that were tied up next to the towpath over the festive period.

A year before she retired she trekked through the snowdrifts with her 16-year-old grandson, which she declared was the worst weather she had encountered in the twenty years she had been doing her Christmas present run. They were on their way to two narrow boat families who were stuck fast in the ice. The iceboat, which was used to clear the way to free the stricken boats, was also unable to move.

When she first started playing Santa Clause, the cost of the Christmas presents came out of her own pocket, but later on she received financial help from several organisations in Northampton including College Street Baptist Church, pupils of Northampton High School for Girls and a group of boy scouts.

In 1951, in recognition of her life of devotion to the boat people, she was awarded the British Empire Medal in the New Year Honours List. She really did not know why she was chosen and when she was first informed, she thought it was an elaborate hoax.

With the coming of nationalisation and the subsequent formation of British Waterways, the company declared in 1956 that Sister Mary in her 70's, was too old to carry on. She was thanked for her services in a ceremony at Southall where she had lunch with the Divisional Manager and was presented with a clock from the company and a silver teapot on behalf of the boat families of the South East Division. She was also given a small pension.

That retirement ceremony made not the slightest break in her work. She affirmed the boat people still needed her and no authority would dictate when she should stop her work.

She kept secret the amount of her pension but did admit that it was not enough even to pay her electricity bills. The sterilisers she now ran on paraffin oil for economy, taking her back to the very beginning again paying for it all herself.

Three years later in April 1959, she had the shock of her life when she was the star of the BBC Television programme *This is Your Life*, which was hosted by Eammon Andrews. The whole country now knew of Sister Mary and the valuable work she was doing.

When a newspaper journalist came to interview her at the surgery in 1962, she told him that he was lucky to find her in. She usually saw between thirty and forty cases every day as well as spending some of her time down the lock on some boat or other (the men carrying her on and off the boat).

Sister Mary carried on for a further six years but her health (a heart condition) at the age of 78 forced her finally to retire. The boat people were stunned at the news and some openly wept, pleading with her to stay, with promises they would look after her.

She moved, with misgivings, to North London to live with her daughter, taking only a few possessions with her and, of course, her surgical instruments. She could not bring herself to talk about paying a return visit, as it would upset her too much.

Sister Mary was not only missed by her beloved boat people but also the many thousands of visitors who saw that very busy uniformed figure by the locks at Stoke Bruerne.

The Florence Nightingale of the canals died in March 1972 in a London hospital at the age of 87 and is buried in the Baptist churchyard at Roade, Northamptonshire.

AELFGIFU OF NORTHAMPTON

(c.996)

A Royal Northamptonian

B ORN ABOUT AD 996 and called 'of Northampton', Aelfgifu was of noble birth and of English or Anglo-Danish stock. She was the daughter of Aelfhelm, Ealdorman (Earl) of York and Wulfruna a lady also of noble birth. The family held large estates of land in Northamptonshire but was principally the ruling family in North Mercia.

In 1006 the family fell from royal favour when King Aethelred suspected them of treachery. As a result, Aelfgifu's father was murdered and her brothers were blinded on royal orders. The family, along with others who were also accused of treachery, became the friends and supporters of the Danish armies in an alliance against King Aethelred.

It was put about that Aelfgifu had been the mistress of King Olaf of Norway, he would have, no doubt, met her when he was in England, but there is no evidence to substantiate the story.

What is certain, however, is that she met the invading Danish leader (Canute) and was chosen to be his wife. It was probable that in early 1014 he claimed marriage with her but when he became King he never made her his Queen. They were driven out of the country soon after and Canute took his new 'wife' to Denmark. They returned to England in late 1015 when Canute, after battling with the Saxons led by Edmund Ironside, was able to take and rule half of England in 1016 with Edmund ruling the other half.

Within a month Edmund mysteriously died, which resulted in Canute becoming the first Dane to become King of England.

Although Aelfgifu did not go through a marriage ceremony with Canute, her position was not regarded in any way as dishonourable, except perhaps by the Church. She was to bear him two sons, Harold Harefoot born probably in Northampton in a palace next to St Peter's Church in about 1015 and Swein about 1016.

In 1017 in order to strengthen his position as King of England, he married Emma the widow of King Aethelred. Although he was still 'married' to Aelfgifu, some commentators assumed she had been his mistress, but she was probably a 'handfast' or common-law wife as was the Danish custom.

Emma, on the other hand, became his formal wife and Queen, making any male children they had, legitimate heirs to the English throne, whilst the children of Aelfgifu were heirs to the throne of Denmark.

There was no love lost between the two women, both being ambitious and aggressive neither wanting their sons to be deprived of the legacy each believed was rightfully theirs.

A scurrilous tale of the time spread, no doubt, to undermine the claims of Aelfgifu for her sons, tells of Aelfgifu not being able to have any children, pretending they were Canute's sons, when in reality Harold was the son of a shoemaker and Swein's a priest. The babes were supposed to have been carried secretly into her bedchamber in bed-warming pans.

For quite some time after Canute's marriage to Emma, there is no mention in the archives of Aelfgifu or her sons. It appears they may have been sent to Denmark, as that is where she and her son Swein next are noted.

Following the death of Harold, King of Denmark (Canute's brother) in 1018, that country was taken by Canute to augment his growing empire. Swein was ordained as his father's Lieutenant over the Wendish region of Denmark but because he was still a minor, Aelfgifu acted as Regent.

In 1028 Canute sailed to Scandinavia with pre-laid plans to take control of Norway from King Olaf. Canute was able to bribe many local chiefs who deserted Olaf forcing him to flee. Taking control, Canute appointed Earl Ericson as Governor of his newly conquered land but he drowned in early 1030 which gave an opportunity for Canute to create his son Swein, King of Norway. Aelfgifu was again appointed Regent as Swein was still in his early teens.

The reign of Swein and Aelfgifu turned out to be a complete fiasco. The Norwegian people having dismissed the oppressive rule of King Olaf, soon found out that they had inherited a far more harsh existence.

Taxation was increased, services due to the Crown were extended and there were severe penalties for acts of violence on these tough northern people. Aelfgifu also introduced Danish customs and officials with power, which further alienated the people. Poor harvests and the resultant famine throughout the land were also blamed on Swein and his mother.

The inevitable revolt came in 1035 when two prominent Norwegian nobles led a force against the unfortunate pair and they were forced to flee, Swein to the court of his half brother Harthacanute in Denmark and Aelfgifu probably to England.

King Canute died 12 November 1035 in Shaftsbury, closely followed by the death of his son Swein. Queen Emma and Aelfgifu both actively sought to gain the English Crown for their respective sons.

The 'Witan' or Government met at Oxford and agreed to make Harold regent of England and by 1037 he had become King. His reign was relatively short, however, as he died 17 March 1040.

With the loss of her other son, Aelfgifu disappears from the records – her fate being lost in the mists of time.

LADY ADELINE OF DEENE PARK

(1824–1915)

Exquisitely eccentric

T HE GLORIOUS SETTING of Deene Park provides the backcloth to the romance of this story, whose village tenants must have been startled by the events taking place up at the big house in the 19th century.

Deene Hall was purchased in 1514 by Sir Robert Brudenell (1461–1531) and passed down the male line of the family. Little of the original house was intact when the prosperous lawyer bought it. His grandson Edmund (1521–1587) built the handsome porch and the Great Hall where, in 1566, Queen Elizabeth I was entertained and partook of dinner.

Edmund was said to have murdered his wife and haunted the upper rooms. However, after a modern conversion, he was never seen again.

His nephew, Thomas, in the next generation, added the sturdy Tower, which he embellished with heraldry. He formed a liaison with another aristocratic family, in marrying the daughter of Sir Thomas Tresham of Rushton Hall, whose son was implicated in the Gunpowder Plot and a compatriot of the infamous Guy Fawkes.

After the traumatic period of the English Civil War, being both a Catholic and a Royalist, he became a fugitive for two years before being committed to the dreaded Tower of London for four years on a charge of high treason. On his succession to the throne, Charles II created him Earl of Cardigan, to compensate for his massive losses, when he had returned to Deene to find his property ransacked. The direct line of inheritance was interrupted here, as his son had died before him.

The estate passed to George, the third Earl, who was young and irresponsible, squandering huge sums of money on entertainment. Being a Protestant, having renounced the Catholic faith, he chose to demolish the chapel. He married a titled lady and restored the house to its former glory, creating a vast lake, which enhanced the view from the house and kept a pack of hounds for the hunt. At the same time, the pair enjoyed living a wildly extravagant lifestyle.

Other members of the family married well, adding to their estates and titles.

James Thomas, the pivot of the next romance, became the seventh Earl of Cardigan (1797–1868) whose fierce ambition was to join the army, in an elite regiment, which he achieved in 1823. He married a divorcee, who subsequently absconded with Lord Colville in 1846.

Tales of his fiery temperament are legendary. Four years earlier, he had fought a bitter duel with a Captain Tuckett on Wimbledon Common, whom he wounded, but not fatally. Lord Cardigan was tried by his peers, at a court martial, but was acquitted.

Dashing and debonair and very much aware of his standing, he fitted out his men, at his own expense, with grand uniforms and flaunted his extravagance. As Major General, he was sent to the Crimean War in 1854 to lead The Charge of the Light Brigade, exhibiting extraordinary valour in the face of danger, riding his beloved charger, Ronald, to become a hero at Balaclava.

Adeline de Horsey (1824–1915) was the wilful daughter of Admiral Spence de Horsey and his spouse, Louisa. The girl spoke several languages and was an accomplished singer and pianist, writing an opera at the age of fifteen!

High-spirited and gregarious, Adeline was presented at Court in 1842, when she was seventeen and soon became betrothed to Count Montemolin, Pretender to the Spanish throne, who was her senior, but she chose to terminate the union.

She mixed with courtesans and the fast set and she was a keen rider to hounds in Quorn country. Very soon, she caught the eye of the captivating seventh Earl at a party at Deene. He was sixty years old at the time, with a certain reputation.

Cardigan was forbidden to visit Adeline in London, by her father, but in defiance, they set up house not far from Park Lane in London and blatantly rode together in fashionable Rotten Row in Hyde Park.

Upon the death of his wife, the Earl rode to inform Adeline and propose marriage, but she did not accept at the time and suggested he observe convention and leave for Ireland!

Regardless of this setback, in 1858 they sailed on his yacht to

Gibraltar and married in style on The Rock. The Governor spurned the new bride and made public his disapproval by having their boat towed out to sea! Queen Isabella of Spain accepted them and they were also granted an audience by Pope Pius IX, riding in a grand carriage to The Vatican.

They finally returned home to Deene to take up their role at the Hall, adding the Ballroom, but were ostracised by society.

The Earl was fond of galloping around the estate on his famous charger, Ronald, whom he had ridden so valiantly in the war, but sadly, the rider was to suffer a fatal fall and died in 1868. He lay in state for two days, until Ronald led the cortège at the funeral to the church, where he would lie among his ancestors.

Adeline, now a widow, continued to lead an outrageous life and took to wearing a blond wig, very much aware of her appearance. She married again, albeit briefly, a Portuguese Count, but it came to nothing as they were incompatible.

She became widely known for her eccentricity, particularly when she ordered her coffin to be made some years before her death, in 1915. Elaborately garbed in her favourite dress of blue silk, she would climb into it to receive her guests, such was their entertainment, but it was, apparently, quite difficult to extricate her torso and had to be hauled out.

Cowes, on the Isle of Wight, was the venue where she spent happier times on the yacht, *Seahorse*, and she would be rowed round the harbour, singing and strumming Italian songs on her guitar. She continued to behave in a scandalous way, being wildly flirtatious, to the extent of chasing the politician Benjamin Disraeli, who scorned her amorous advances.

Often to be seen cycling around the estate, she wore her late husband's regimental uniform, the scarlet trousers and 'cheeky-bum' jacket, which he had worn in battle. She appeared in their old stomping-ground in Hyde Park, in her gold wig and a tricorn hat, embroidered coat and leopard skin, accompanied by an escort, increasingly bizarre in her behaviour to the end of her life.

A bronze equestrian statuette of Adeline, by Sir Edgar Bourne and a picture of Lord Cardigan riding into battle at Balaclava exists. The preserved head of charger, Ronald, in a glass-case, who survived his master by many years, along with the magnificent uniforms, have been retained within the Hall.

The effigy of Lord Cardigan lies in the Church of St. Peter, alongside those of his ancestors.

An elderly resident of nearby Stanion, as a 96-year-old lady (now deceased), as a young girl, described Lord Cardigan as 'dashing from Deene Hall in a carriage with postillions on his way to Kettering railway station' and assumed he was about to join his regiment to lead the battle which was to become immemorable in the annals of British history – The Charge of the Light Brigade.

After the Second World War, the late Mrs George Brudenell used to ride her bicycle along the endless corridors of the Hall in order to reach the far kitchens!

ANNIE LOUISA BAGSHAW

(1866–1960)

*A tribute to Grannie Annie –
'a tidy little body'*

ANNIE LOUISA WAS A LADY, in every sense of the word, of diminutive stature, who always wore light gloves in summer and dark ones in winter, whenever she left the house.

Her spring hats were of straw and in the winter, of felt, but were annually trimmed with artificial violets and clusters of bright cherries,

crowning wispy white hair, with a bun under a gossamer hairnet. Her outdoor coats were long and severe, skimming black side-buttoned boots, whose essential buttonhook hung on a nail beside the scullery door. Thick stockings were beneath dark, sprigged dresses with high necks, often with a discreet frill and always fastened by a gold filigree brooch or an antique cameo.

Married for the third time late in life (she told her close friends that she was 'a late

*Annie Louisa and Richard Bagshaw.
Courtesy: Mia Butler.*

77

developer') to Richard Bagshaw, a prominent businessman, who operated a number of charabancs (which preceded buses) and a haulage firm with a fleet of lorries.

Living with them in Kettering, was her older sister Polly, a semi-invalid and another younger sister Flo, who was a spinster and genteel ladies' companion. The trio, all born within ten years of each other, always referred to themselves as 'we girls', even when they were all over eighty!

Husband and wife were both Guardians of the Poor Law Institution (now St Mary's Hospital) in Kettering, and both were highly respected in their day. They took their duties very seriously, never missing committee meetings and weekly visits. They were financially able to provide for the inmates Christmas Party, where each received sweets, an orange or twist of 'baccy' and Woodbine cigarettes. The summer outing saw the excited folk piling into the 'charas' for a long journey to the seaside on solid tyres. These were highlights of the year for the less fortunate and must have sometimes bewildered other day trippers!

Annie Louisa was of the most compassionate nature and would make her weekly 'rounds' of the institution, visiting unwed mothers and their babies, and was always concerned with their welfare. She would tour the laundry, inspect the washing and the massive chunks of carbolic soap used on the washboards, even the suds in the dollytubs. Great iron mangles with lethal wooden rollers squelched the water from endless sheets every day in this oppressive steamy atmosphere.

This tiny woman would accompany the portly Matron, who was garbed in a starched cap and apron about her ample form, plus a huge bunch of keys dangling from the waist. Her husband was Master in charge of the males. The daily rounds of inspection meticulously checking all aspects of the workhouse.

The pair lived in rather a grand house in the grounds, where a polite tea was served by a maid at the conclusion of the afternoon.

Poor Law Institutions in the 1930s took in tramps and vagrants of both sexes, who were scrubbed, fed and watered and treated for fleas and nits, with ample supplies of Jeyes Fluid and each allocated to an iron bedstead with a lumpy flock mattress.

Families in reduced circumstances, bereaved or abandoned, were not turned away. The few who were able to work were given modest jobs for meagre pocket money.

Business people of the town gave of their time and money until such establishments ceased, prior to the Welfare State.

When on a visit to her friends in Gretton, Annie Louisa introduced a young girl to April Fool's Day, by sending her to the local dairy with a tin can, for 'a pint of pigeon's milk'. She had a sense of humour too, though she had no children of her own, but several by marriage, who all loved her unconditionally.

Grannie Annie was born December 1866 and died May 1960.

ON A VERY PERSONAL NOTE

Harking back, though not quite to the Victorian age, I must have been foisted on to the diminutive Annie Louisa and grandfather Richard at about the age of three years, but I remember nothing of the transition. My mother had disappeared and bravely (in retrospect) ALB, on her third marriage and herself childless, must have taken on a difficult and wayward child, who was not even a blood relative.

My memories are of those two loving guardians and a working father, who lived in the house next door and only joined us for dinner at one o'clock.

The dining table was always immaculate, with a pristine starched linen tablecloth and unpretentious but monogrammed silver cutlery always polished and never tarnished. Shiny water glasses and crystal water jug and a silver cruet. At tea time an oblong brass crumb-tray with an ebony handle and matching soft bristle brush was used to sweep up any crumbs. Shaking a large white cloth outside the back door was probably not practical, though the perfume of the dainty white jasmine on the wall was a delight – but not in the midst of winter!

Pink Japanese wind-flowers nodded in the garden and a mass of crocus flowers and snowdrops heralded spring and I remember how the birds used to peck at the base of each yellow bud, to sup the sweet nectar. Bright marigolds were popular then and deep purple flags (irises) and japonica leaned against the brick wall. The house was graced by a Virginia creeper, which turned a glorious scarlet as the year went on, leaving bare stems when the leaves fell – until the next time round.

The air-raid shelter did nothing to enhance the view, so it was conveniently banished to my father's less-orderly garden next door! Masses of pink old-fashioned sweet peas and bushes of hydrangeas, where I used to plant rusty nails around the base to change the colour from pink to blue – or was it the reverse?

The rope wash-line (not yet retractable) was strung between two poles over the grass lawn, frequently cut by the gardener, an old 'retainer'.

The house was large and the front entrance tiled in Victorian design, with steps up from the avenue, sticky from the residue of the mature lime trees in summer. The front door had stained glass panels and a highly-polished brass knocker, opening to a long hall right through to the back kitchen and scullery.

There was a fussy dark-red stair carpet fixed by brass rods and an elaborate hat stand with a little square mirror, for sticks, umbrellas, coats and hats, a boot-rack and some sombre flocked wallpaper in the hall, hung with two brass warming pans.

The front room was used only in the evenings after work was done, when ALB and her infirm sister Polly, would sit on hard velvet chairs with antimacassars and embroidered footstools. A massive sideboard reaching almost to the ceiling, housed the 'best' china (only washed at spring cleaning) and bore hideous ornaments and a fluted pink glass fruit bowl, never filled, and small mahogany side-tables for the work baskets. A brass companion set in the hearth, of course, and the daily chore on a winter's morning was to clear the ashes and set a new fire for the evening. A red-patterned carpet with a dizzy border on the floor and lacy curtains at the bay window and a quivering fringe around the lampshade.

Grampy Richard had his own study, very much the male domain, where one knocked before entering, even to say 'goodnight'. There was a huge table for his ledgers, for the family haulage business and early charabancs and later, several buses were added to the fleet in addition to lorries. The former, operating country services around the villages. He had very regular hours through the day, emerging only for meals, though there was a door to the garden, which occasionally stood ajar, perhaps to clear the air of clouds of smoke from his ancient pipe. At nine every evening, he lit a Cuban cigar before leaving in a carefully pressed pinstripe suit, usually navy, a flower in his buttonhole and a freshly brushed smart bowler hat, to step into the waiting Humber Snipe, driven by my father, to the Conservative Club and always returned exactly one hour later!

Grannie Annie was an excellent cook and dinner at one consisted of a two or three-course meal of meat, vegetable and always a pudding. There might be tripe and onions (ugh!) steak and kidney pie or suet pudding in a basin, liver and bacon, oxtail soup, braised rabbit, jugged hare made with port wine, as well as other traditional meats. In wartime, a share in a pig provided us with extra fare. We had a vast kitchen garden and orchard elsewhere, neatly defined by low hedges, which provided a constant supply of vegetables and luscious fruits, such as loganberries. Extensive asparagus beds were denuded of their succulent spears by the gardener and banded into neat bundles tied with raffia, every day in season.

Always scrumptious puddings, steaming basins with spotted dick, all kinds of suet 'clangers', every kind of milk pudding from semolina to tapioca (cat's-eyes!) and rice with nutmeg on top, stewed fruits and jugs of thick yellow custard or perhaps cream from the milkman, delivered from his little 'trap' as a special treat.

For 'high tea' on Sundays, there would be ham sliced from a whole leg, or fresh salmon with salad or a crusty pork pie. Home made Victoria sponge, fruitcake rich and dark and probably wobbly jelly from a mould. We even made our own cream cheese with sour milk hung in a fold of muslin over a basin in the pantry and my own favourite, curds and whey.

There was game in season, pheasant, partridge, wild duck and a gigantic turkey at Christmas. These all came into the scullery in feather and were plucked and drawn over a tin bath then singed over the gas cooker, by Grampy Richard, evoking the festive season.

Upstairs each bedroom had a fireplace, but seldom used except perhaps in the case of extreme illness. Vast feather eiderdowns and pillows made the beds cosy, especially the feather beds, plumped up every morning (as soon as one was big enough!) and woollen blankets with pink ribboned edges. Prayers were said kneeling on a thin rug beside the bed, regardless of the ice forming on the inside of the windowpanes. A chamber pot would be tucked under the springs.

A brown pot hot water bottle or one of ribbed aluminium, helped on a wintry night, but was impossible to touch and was gingerly dropped into an old knitted sock for protection. Chilblains were a constant problem and Snowflake ointment was lavishly anointed to this end.

The bath was enamel, standing on iron legs and a scary temperamental gas boiler for the weekly ablutions and the lino pretty chilly to the bare feet!

I went first to a little private school, Miss Pink's, at the age of about five, to absorb the crucial patterns of behaviour. Good manners were obligatory, as well as the basic subjects or reading, writing and arithmetic. Things changed and I loathed the 'big school', the milling children, the navy serge gymslips, blouse and school tie. Grannie Annie sewed a pocket on to my voluminous navy gym knickers to accommodate a raw square of camphor 'to ward off colds' – humiliating!

DR GRACE THORNTON

(1913–1987)

A woman in a man's world

Dr GRACE THORNTON was a highly respected, ebullient woman who made her name in diplomatic circles, accepting great responsibility, exhibiting determination, valour and achievement in her chosen career.

Clara Grace was born 27 June 1913, the only daughter of Alderman A A Thornton, one of Kettering's early Mayors, and his wife, along with brothers John and Pat, soon after the town was elevated to Borough status. Her father was the founder of a leading jewellery shop, which still flourishes in the town centre.

Grace was educated at Kettering High School, but had perhaps already set foot on the ladder of her distinguished rise to prominence when she won a competition promoted by the League of Nations, for an essay on that subject. When she returned from claiming her prize, a scholarship to summer school, she was fired with enthusiasm and great aspirations.

Early in her formative years, Grace was considered to play the part of Ophelia on stage, but her

Courtesy: Loaned by Mavis Thornton.

teacher thought that her work in preparation for the School Certificate might be disrupted.

Evidently already concerned with social issues, as a schoolgirl, she was to voice her opinion on the fact that an unfair example of male preference even then, was that "girls had to pay 2d extra for their (school) badges, on top of the boy's 6d".

She went to Cambridge University in 1932 in Newnham College where she continued her studies. She became a Fellow, achieving in 1935, the first woman to gain a double first in her subjects of Archaeology and Anthropology. She was awarded the University Scandinavian Studentship in the following two years and in the next, attained her Ph.D on the Book of the Settlement of Iceland, her research project.

During the years of World War II, her first job was based in London, through the ravages of the Blitz, when she took up a position as a secretary in the Ministry of Information. Her superiors at that time were Margaret Thatcher and Barbara Castle. She was also involved, for a spell, in the closely-kept secret enclave of Bletchley Park, working with the code-breakers, more lately revealed to the outside world.

She joined the Copenhagen Embassy as press attaché, before transferring to the British Legation in Reykjavik in Iceland, in the post of Vice-Consul, in which capacity she was able to explore further the volcanic island and its history. Her brilliant linguistic skills enabled her to translate two books by the celebrated Hans Christian Andersen. Returning next to Copenhagen and then to Brussels, in the early 1960s.

As Consul General of Djakarta in Indonesia in 1963, when the founding of Malaysia was the root cause of disturbing unrest and civil disobedience was rife, the Embassy was looted and burned. Arsonists had discovered details of British residents and had destroyed their properties. The British nationals became isolated in the Shell oilfields of Borneo and were in dire straits. This brave lady flew there in the face of fierce opposition, arranging an airlift for more than a hundred civilians, before returning to Singapore, where she modestly disclaimed her personal involvement.

On her return to the United Kingdom, Dr Thornton was interviewed on television by John Freeman, displaying reticence regarding her activities, but admitted that she suffered the worst bout of dysentery in her entire life. The Times reported her as "unflappable, splendidly outspoken and fiercely formidable" and another article in the same newspaper labelled her "a woman in a man's world".

A further posting ensued to Lisbon, as Consular-General, for the next five years, before returning to the Foreign Office in charge of the Consular Department.

Her housekeeper, in referring to her mistress, said that when a tricky situation arose, she was enough "to frighten the horses". She had a great sense of humour when her presence would allow and was ever the consummate advocate of women's issues. She was undaunted, effective and admired in a male dominated society and remained unmarried throughout her peripatetic life. Her leisure interests were given as music, embroidery, Scandinavia and cats!

Dr Thornton published two books of her own and was the recipient of diverse honours in her lifetime for her diplomatic skills, as listed:

Scandinavian Studentship Award 1936/37
The Danish Freedom Medal
Knight of the Order of Drannenbrog
Order of the Icelandic Falcon 1983
Order of the British Empire 1959
Commander of the Order of the British Empire 1964
Member of the Royal Victorian Order

In her retirement in 1963, in London, Dr Thornton devoted her considerable energies to her work as Secretary of the Women's National Commission at the Foreign Office until 1978.

After her death at St Stephen's Hospital, Chelsea, on 27 June 1987, at a memorial service to celebrate her life, the Bishop of Gibraltar in Europe, gave the address, a fitting tribute to a career diplomat of outstanding ability.

LADY ETHEL WICKHAM
OF COTTERSTOCK HALL
(1864–1961)

A gracious lady

CHARLES, 10th Marquis of Huntly was Chief of the Clan of the Gordons, of French Ancestry, who was twice wed and sired seven sons and seven daughters. His second wife, Antoinetta Pegus bore their last child, Ethelreda, soon after his death in 1863.

Huntly	1847	Mary
Lewis	1848–1870	Evelyn
Bertrand	1850–1869	Grace
Douglas	1850–1869	Margaret
Esme	1853–1900	Elena
Granville	1856–1907	Edith
Randolf	born and died 1859	Ethelreda 1864–1961
		m. Henry Wickham

Milestones written by the 11th Marquis of Huntly reveals an intriguing insight into the life of aristocratic country families of the period and gives a lively account of the Braemar Gathering in Scotland in 1861 and of their family estate at Aboyne. Also mentioned is the first day of the Penny Post introduced in 1840, when letters were dispatched at the uniform rate of one penny, one of these being sent to his grandparents adorned by the sender with a comic drawing.

Lady Ethel was born 31 January 1864 at Orton Longueville, in Huntingdon and was given the name of Ethelreda, consequently taking the shortened version, but was never to know her father who died before her birth. As a child she joined her sisters, who were educated by a French governess and from an early age, studied music.

Lady Ethel Wickham. Courtesy: Loaned by John Simpson.

In her adult life, she displayed great devotion to nursing and when a serious epidemic of influenza swept the county and devastated the village of Barnwell, she was likened to Florence Nightingale, in her concern for the stricken.

She was influential in the initial organisation of the Northamptonshire District Nursing Association, founded in 1903, of which she was President for 43 years, and only ceased when the local authority took it over.

One of her close friends and neighbours, Lady Lilford over at Lilford Hall nearby, collaborated with Lady Ethel, who shared her interest and together they inaugurated the North Northamptonshire Music Festival, in which they became actively involved for their lifetimes.

Married at the age of nineteen years to Colonel Henry Wickham, who hailed from Yorkshire roots, the couple first lived at Alwalton Hall, moving to Barnwell Castle, before eventually settling at Cotterstock Hall near to Oundle. In 1912, the house was entirely lit by paraffin oil lamps, preferred by the lady of the house. Colonel Wickham was a gallant soldier who fought several campaigns overseas in World War I and was to die in 1933.

Lady Ethel became a prominent figure in the county, with her vibrant personality and came to the fore socially with a flair for organising grand banquets and a variety of entertainments. She was a keen shot with a rifle and a fearless horsewoman and hunter, keeping horses in her own stables at the Hall and other venues. She frequently rode with the Cottesmore and Quorn Hunts, in addition to following the Fitzwilliam Hounds, whose descendant pack exists to this day, as well as over at Melton Mowbray.

Richard III granted the right to hunt in Rockingham Forest, to the Abbot of Peterborough in the 14th century. The current pack comprises sturdy hounds bred from the original line and are now kennelled in the sham ruin or folly dating from 1767, on the Milton Park Estate, after their quarters were destroyed by fire in the 19th century.

She took pleasure in riding a bicycle and later a motorcycle, given to her by Lord Lonsdale, her brother-in-law.

Come foul weather or fine, this formidable woman could often be seen striding over the countryside around Cotterstock, Tansor or Ashton, regardless of season!

It is said that other customers in Oundle were sometimes left to wait impatiently in Percy Amp's grocery shop (himself a churchwarden and robust man in attire and habit), whilst the lady was attended, such was her magnetism and charisma! Known too, for her impeccable dress sense and style, whatever the occasion, even when riding her bicycle or motorbike.

Lady Ethel, sporting an old felt hat and smock, had an abiding passion for her garden, where she chose to introduce new species of trees. Assisted by Mr Moore, her faithful lifelong devoted gardener, their work was reflected in the splendid flowerbeds and lawns.

Toward the close of her busy life, she was elected President of the Peterborough Agricultural Show at the age of 94 years, which she graciously accepted, to the delight of her many admirers.

Her daughter Molly, the last of her children to be born, also had a gift of concern for the staff, who were permitted to visit fetes and festivals to perform folk dances at Lilford, Elton and Deene Halls. These employees also respected the gentlemanly ways of good manners of her father, Colonel Wickham.

The demise of Lady Ethel in May 1961, caused the Hall to be sold, which has since passed out of the family.

DAME EDITH SITWELL

(1887–1964)

A doyen of sensibilities

COMMITTING WORDS TO PAPER seems alarmingly inadequate to one who knows little of Edith Sitwell's work, yet must acknowledge her as a legendary eccentric of her time. This must be a personal summation of this vital poet. Lecturer, critic, and artist and no disrespect is intended by my limited knowledge of the vast accumulation of her mastery of the written and spoken word.

A poignant visit to her grave, several years ago, on the rim of the cemetery annexe of St Mary's Church at Weedon Lois (a church with an unusual history of its own), brings the visitor to the tall sombre headstone, bearing a bronze sculptured image on a plaque, by the celebrated artist Henry Moore. It illustrates a pair of hands representing youth and age – the span of life. Inscribed beneath are the closing lines of her own poem *The Wind of Early Spring*:

> *The past and present are as one – Accordant and Discordant,*
> *Youth and Age, and death and birth.*
> *For out of one comes all – From all comes one.*

Beyond the metal fence, there is a wide view of quiet pastures and a trace of medieval fishponds from previous centuries.

Her devoted brother, Sacheverell and his wife Georgina lived close by at Weston Hall, with whom Edith often stayed. Both are buried here together with his mother Lady Ida Sitwell.

The only daughter to be born to her aristocratic parents, Sir George and Lady Ida Sitwell, on 7 September 1887, at Wood End, Scarborough, she was the eldest child. Two brothers followed, Osbert and Sacheverell, completing the family. All were destined to become literary prodigies.

Their grandmother was the daughter of the Duke of Beaufort and her great grandmother, the Duchess of Troy, from whom Edith thought she had inherited her 'Byzantine eyes' and that she bore a marked resemblance, with her exquisite bone structure and elegant hands, to Queen Elizabeth I.

Was she introvert as a child, appearing grave and withdrawn into her own world? Her adult recollections of events from childhood, tell of distress, misunderstandings and the disapproval of her parents, against which she rebelled. Her later poems frequently hark back to emphasise her unhappiness.

There are many references to her great grandmother, the Duchess of Troy, of seaside holidays to improve the child's health, along with her aunts who were 'tall as pagodas' and Punch and Judy shows on the beach. Tales from Troy Castle figure prominently in her prose.

Her other grandmother is seen in quite different terms, even described as 'like an alien being', yet much more in touch with daily life and caught up in the more prosaic minutiae or routine.

Brother Osbert wrote of his sister's deprivation of their mother's love, for he was acutely aware of being the favourite and felt that harm might be caused to the girl's nervous system, through certain restrictions.

As a teenager, she was taken to the Italian castle Montegufori, purchased by her father as a winter retreat for the family, travelling, perhaps tediously, by train.

She ran away to the Isle of Wight, with her maid, to

Dame Edith's headstone with plaque by Henry Moore at Weedon Lois.

take a dramatic visit to Swinburn's grave, whose poems she had discovered and become enamoured.

Helen Rootham, herself a talented poet and translator, became Edith's tutor and made a considerable impact on the girl's life and indeed, opened the door to the wonders of another world, of concerts and galleries. She was introduced to the great French artists of the century, alerting her of things to come, fanning that already creative spark into flames.

1922 onward seems to have been a highly prolific period for Edith's writings, and revealing facets of her personality, unfold and some puzzling and odd glimpses of her thoughts surface in *My Awkward Moments* of 1927.

Helen Rootham became her close companion and made it possible for Edith to develop her potential. Together, they moved away from the countryside to a modest flat in Bayswater, on an upper floor of the Victorian, Pembridge Mansions in 1914, just prior to the beginning of the World War 1.

Artists vied for her favours and she had her portrait painted. Photographers were dazzled by her singular looks and Cecil Beaton photographed her in a coffin, in exotic attire in bed attended by a negress and numerous bizarre poses.

Her series *Portraits* and *The English Eccentrics* reveal fascinating cameos of personalities known to her. Not only was she seen as brilliant by her admirers, but also had a physically haunting aura about her, tall, dark and mysterious, with hooded all-seeing eyes. Her dress was equally startling, favouring hats, silks and brocades, sheepskin and flowing ankle-length skirts, all of which enhanced the drama about her persona. She must have been perceived as daunting to those not privileged to be in her presence. Her life became immersed in the city beat of the artistic crowd, where the famous and infamous sought invitations to her legendary teas (yet some were reported in a scathing manner!). Many regarded her with curiosity and she referred to herself as 'a spiritual adventurer'.

She became editor of *Wheels* an anthology of original verse in 1916, which she carried on for the next five years. In this role, she met and entertained a multitude of poets, both established and aspiring, the latter perhaps fawning or currying to win her favours.

Edith published an avalanche of poems, her first in 1926, one publicly performed against a background of music by William Walton. A blizzard of poetry and prose ensued, elevating her status even further.

Her *Modern Values* clearly expressed her views in an article written for The Spectator and a piece for the Sunday Express written in 1928 *Must the World be so Noisy?* (even more apt for today) are both charming and provocative works. Her series *Portraits* covers a whole gamut of persons, from barmaids to Tennyson, with such intriguing titles such as *Pastor – takes the Restaurant Car to Heaven.*

In the middle years, Helen Rootham, in 1930, was diagnosed with cancer, from which she succumbed eight years later. Edith took on a great deal of responsibility for the care of her friend, then turning to prose rather than poetry, eventually to return to the latter.

Some Observations on Women's Poetry tells that it should be 'elegant as a peacock', among other things! As a lecturer, she must have been rivetting – or even spellbinding!

Following several lecture tours with brother Osbert, from 1948, to America, she returned to London in 1954 to be honoured with the award of Dame of the British Empire, in addition to the four honorary doctorates for literature received from Leeds, Durham, Sheffield and Oxford Universities.

The next year she became a Roman Catholic and was admitted to their church.

The Aldeburgh Festival of 1957 was the setting of the first meeting of Edith and Elizabeth Salter, an Australian, who was to become her devoted friend and secretary for the rest of her life. Already a novelist, further publications appeared as time progressed, in addition to two biographies and Elizabeth's own memoir *The Last Years of the Rebel.*

During a brief spell in Paris, with Elizabeth, Edith found a kindred spirit in Gertrude Stein and met other leading figures, such as Picasso and Matisse, before returning to London, soon to become a novelist herself.

Taken Care Of, an anthology published after Edith's demise in 1964, is a look at her impending death. How can one describe Edith Sitwell? An enigma, self-contained, dynamic, expressive, sarcastic, lethal, critical, obscure, melodramatic, pious, often wounding and an acerbic wit? Surely, a genius!

KATHLEEN LILIAN 'BILL' COGGINS

(1909–1994)

An aptitude for athletics

THE YOUNGEST OF SEVEN CHILDREN born to James Chambers and his wife of Raunds in 1909, Kathleen grew up affectionately known as 'Bill'.

In her early years she attended Wellingborough High School, cycling from her home in the village to Higham Ferrers station, where she caught a train to Wellingborough, to walk up the long hill each morning. She left in 1924, already showing promise as an athlete. She became involved with her father's heel-manufacturing business at the age of fourteen, to eventually become Managing Director, from which position she retired after 54 years, in 1977.

A fit and keen runner, which she had taken up at twenty-one, originally to assist a friend in training, developed into a passion and a most successful part of her exacting daily routine.

Bill married Arthur Coggins in 1933, who was later to join the family business. Wed only recently and unknown to her, Arthur entered her into a race at Blackpool on Easter Monday. She easily became a winner of the Midlands Women's AAA Championships of both 100 and 220 yards in 1933 and the previous year. Her record time for this prestigious event remained unbroken for ten years. Her training in the Raunds Harriers already established locally.

Selected to join the Northants County Hockey 2nd XI, she toured with them in Germany, when her enthusiasm for the game prompted her to found the Raunds Women's Hockey Club, aided by Arthur, as referee, who was to die in 1973.

Listed in *Who's Who in Sport of 1935*, an authoritative reference guide to sport and sportsmen, Bill's attributes read:

> *Captain and Treasurer Raunds Ladies Hockey, Captain Northants County Hockey 2nd XI, Chairman Ladies Section Raunds and District Harriers, Midland Counties Women's AAA 1932 and 1933, 100 and 220 yards Champion. Winner of 28 prizes in 3 seasons.*

It is interesting to note, in the same guide, an advertisement for tennis gear:

> *Davis Cup Model 'C' tennis racket 55/-, Tournament Model Complete with grip 67/6. Used by prominent Tournament Players Throughout the World. Also The Championship Regd. Tennis Ball with the MORE THAN DOUBLE SUPAPILE COVER.*

In those days, top prizes were often of goods, which made a valuable addition to the home of the newly-weds. The couple were steadily accumulating a vast 'bottom drawer' of household items such as furnishings, fine crockery and a handsome pewter tea-set! The

'Bill' with trophies galore! Courtesy: Sheila Carr.

accompanying photograph illustrates the diversity of these well-earned rewards.

Bill continued to compete for several years until she had two children, one son and a daughter, though still playing energetic tennis.

She became heavily involved during World War II, organising Raunds Spitfire Week and a series of ballroom lessons and dances, to a duo of musicians. She served on the local charities committee, with fundraising and sporting events. As President of the local branch of British Legion, she took on the responsibility for the Poppy Day Appeal. Money was raised to convert an old chapel room for functions such as the Badminton Club, all these efforts bringing people together.

Aided by her husband, President of Raunds Temperance Band, they organised a successful sponsored walk to raise cash for new uniforms for the bandsmen, who were competing in the National Brass Band Championship.

Not one to settle into sedentary retirement, Bill later travelled alone to visit relatives in New Zealand, Australia and an adventurous trip in America on a Greyhound bus, revelling in a stunning flight through the splendours of the Grand Canyon.

Remembered fondly as an accomplished athlete, loving mother, businesswoman and tireless worker in the community, Bill's name will not easily be forgotten in Raunds.

LADY DIANA SPENCER

(1710–1735)

The first of that name

DIANA SPENCER, the first Lady Di, was born to the Countess of Sunderland, formerly Anne Churchill, one of the four beautiful sisters, all of whom were ladies-in-waiting to Queen Anne. Anne Churchill became the second wife of Charles Spencer, 3rd Earl of Sunderland, already with a young family from his previous marriage.

At the time of Diana's birth, the family home was Sunderland House in Piccadilly, London.

Their grandmother, Sarah Churchill, the Duchess of Marlborough, formed a very close relationship with Diana right from the start, which lasted until the young woman's untimely demise. The Earl of Sunderland referred to his daughter as 'poor little Dear Dye' after her mother's sudden death in 1716, who was laid to rest in the family vault at the church of St Mary the Virgin at Great Brington on the Althorp estate in Northamptonshire.

The country seat of the Spencer family is at Althorp where Diana spent much of her earlier years, together with elder brothers, Charles and Johnny, though little between them in age, along with their peers, played in the nursery and out and about in the spacious parkland.

The Duchess of Marlborough, wife of John Churchill, first Duke of Marlborough, took Diana on as her responsibility, as the child's own father was frequently involved in other business elsewhere. Diana travelled around during her short life between Marlborough House in London, Hollywell House in St Albans, and later Blenheim Palace, at a time when carriages were uncomfortable and the roads hazardous. Visits were made cross-country to their relatives, the Montagu family, at Boughton House, near Kettering.

The bond between the generations was exceedingly strong and Diana helped with her elder's correspondence, when the Duchess referred to her as 'Secretary of State', and is attributed to saying of the young girl "Lady Die too perfect to be described".

It was soon time to consider suitors for the budding young Diana, now almost 20, of which there was no shortage, including the possibility of an alliance with the Prince of Wales. Several proposals of marriage were received, considered and rejected, as Diana was of high birth and prospect, and a reciprocal gentleman of equal status was desirable. Early in the New Year, the Duchess gave a ball to select candidates for this purpose.

Lord John Russell was the most likely champion for her hand and they duly met at his father's residence at Woburn. They were soon wed by special licence, witnessed by only by a small elite company, thought to have gathered at Marlborough House, close to where our late Princess Diana spent her last night as a commoner before her marriage to Charles, the Prince of Wales.

Lord and Lady Russell's London home was in Gresham Street, but they journeyed extensively, including the new Blenheim Palace as well as the supervision of their new home at Cheam and dealing with family machinations.

Diana gave premature birth to a baby son, John, after an accident when she was thrown from her carriage. Sadly, later that day, John died. At about the same time her husband became the 4th Duke of Bedford on the demise of his brother, but news of his death travelled slowly and did not arrive until after their son was laid to rest in the family vault at Chenies in Buckinghamshire.

Diana's concern for her grandmother's health and indeed, her own, continued, when she was convinced she was pregnant again. Both ladies, with such firm ties, were ill at the same period, hindering their affectionate visits to each other.

Diana died in a weakened state, at the tender age of 26 years, having contracted consumption (tuberculosis) and was laid to rest in the Bedford's Chapel in the Church of St Michael at Chenies.

Her grandmother, the ailing Duchess, lingered on in declining health, to die in 1744.

The two namesakes had led similar lives of tragedy and trauma, each admired for their beauty, elegance and aristocratic poise, and the common bond of their childhood spent at Althorp House.

MARIA VON SANDIZELL

(1805–1902)

A Continental lady

MARIA ELISABETH VON SANDIZELL 1805–1902, was a lady with comparatively exotic and aristocratic lineage, daughter of Count Thomas Sandizell, a Bavarian nobleman.

She attended boarding school from seven to seventeen years, which was run along the lines of a seat of learning founded by Napoleon in France and was considered suited to her status. Petite and dainty, she was, in due course, presented at Court, as her position in society demanded.

In Munich, she met the debonair and youthful English diplomat, Thomas Cartwright, in his capacity as Secretary to the English Legation. The father of Thomas, William Ralph Cartwright, raised a number of objections to his son's choice of a wife. Of prime concern was that the young woman was a Catholic, where his family was of the Protestant faith. When the couple were granted permission to marry by the Pope, the nuptials were no longer denied.

They were married abroad in 1824 and initially lived in Munich, where their first-born son Willy was delivered. Until that time, the males in the Cartwright family had wed their English equals, but such was the success of this union, there soon followed other foreign alliances.

Four years on, leaving the Continent behind and her ancestral home beside the Danube in vast forests, Thomas brought them to Aynho to meet his large family of twelve other siblings, of which he was the eldest.

At that time, Lili began a diary, in which she recorded her observations of domesticity, family life, religion and expressions of politics in a new country. Penned by her hand in French, this exercise was to continue for the rest of her life.

It was to be six more years before Lili made her second visit to Aynhoe House, bringing Tommy, her second son, but without her husband, who had taken up a position in Brussels and had kept Willy with him there.

One of the many legacies and attributes Lili left behind was a sizeable collection of perceptive watercolours graphically illustrating the mansion, pictures of the hall, study, dining room, library, conservatory, kitchen, brew house, laundry, landings and the austere cold bathroom. On the upper floors were a number of bedrooms and a nursery.

Julia, William Ralph's second wife shared Lili's artistic and enthusiastic passion, both being talented painters and produced exterior views of the surrounding park and estate, where Aynhoe House perches on the Jurassic limestone ridge on the edge of the Cherwell Valley.

Life with the copious ménage was sometimes tedious for Lili, who had been more exposed to the Continental courts and a more genteel and sophisticated way of life. She was constantly surrounded by a mass of family and their friends and took refuge in her diary and art.

There were duty visits to make, as the social order of standing was closely observed. Forays into the village, the most southerly in the county, where cottages were often sparse and cold inside, being built of honey-coloured stone with thatched roofs. Every garden grew an apricot tree, a legacy from feudal times, when the lord of the manor took fruit from his tenants in part payment of their rent. Many of the folk were skilled lace-makers, as was quite common in rural communities.

The manor house had been originally acquired by a lawyer, Robert Cartwright, whose ancestral roots were in Cheshire. Occupied in the English Civil War by the defeated Royalists, who razed it to the ground, whilst the owner, at that time a Parliamentarian, was absent in London.

Following several major changes and additions over the ensuing years, Lili continued to painstakingly record all aspects of the estate, leaving behind a splendid cameo of this Victorian household.

She had many anxieties, not least, the fervent wish to rejoin the other half of her close family. Eventually, in 1835, she was able to fulfill her desire and journeyed to Frankfurt, where her relatives sometimes came to visit, much to her delight. She was then within reach of her own family seat and was able to keep in constant touch, between entertaining dignitaries and indulge in more cultural pursuits.

A transfer to Sweden created new challenges at the Court of the Swedish King and his Queen.

Both boys, now grown, were expected to continue their education in England, at Oxford, but all did not bode well and another trip to Aynho followed, where marriages among the younger set were being planned.

William Cartwright died in 1847, when his eldest son Thomas, succeeded as heir and Lili was elevated to become mistress of the house and in the continued absence of her husband in Stockholm, communication was difficult. Again, she turned to her painting to produce a further sequence of pictures and when her widowed stepmother Julia moved to a new home, she felt the loss of her friend and ally.

Lili became ill with all the worry and responsibility now placed upon her and sought the benefit of the mineral waters at nearby Astrop. She made the tedious journey to London to visit her personal physician and was able to revive her keen interest in the French theatre and meet with Royal acquaintances.

Reunited with all her family, the problems were not yet over, as Willy announced his marriage to what his mother considered 'an unworthy person' and this caused an unhealable rift.

Sir Thomas died in 1850 at the age of 79 years, when his son Willy inherited Aynhoe and Tommy married an heiress from Scotland.

Aynhoe House was commandeered by the army, for the second time in World War II and the spacious parkland desecrated by a massive petrol store, where Italian prisoners-of-war had the task of felling and dismantling the dilapidated Nissen huts in order to bring some semblance of order and restoration.

Wrought-iron grave marker of Marie Elisabeth August Cartwright. Courtesy: Mia Butler.

The elegant Aynhoe House stands within the park, visible from the road which curves away over the hilltop, as the River Cherwell wends its way below between water meadows, to the gentle folds of the distant Cotswolds.

The property passed out of the family ownership into private hands in 1960.

In the churchyard of St Michael's is a highly ornate wrought iron grave marker, with a shield on the central column beneath a coronet, denoting the rank of the occupant. It bears the inscription 'Here lies the body of Marie Elisabeth August Cartwright eldest daughter of Captain Count Sandizell, Bavaria and widow of the late Sir Thomas Cartwright GCH Born Feb 20th 1805 Died April 13th 1902 RIP'.

MISS CECIL WILSON MacQUEEN

(Dates unknown)

'Be Prepared' – Girl Guide motto

M ISS CECIL MACQUEEN was highly respected within the Girl Guide movement. Known with affection to her friends as 'Queenie', her life and that of her mother, who acted as Quarter-Master for County Camps and died in 1940, was devoted to this worthy organisation and by example, showed that 'nothing less than perfection will do'.

The Thrapston Brownies and Guides, not far from her residence at Wadenhoe House, benefitted greatly from her wide experience and she went on to become County Camp Advisor and later, Midland Area Assistant to Head of Camping for England. In addition, she held Warrants as District and Division Commissioner for almost thirty years, receiving too, the highest cherished award that could be given in 1954, the Beaver.

Thrapston Girl Guides with Miss MacQueen. Courtesy: The late Anne Beasley.

101

Sound advice, for which she was often remembered, would be "there's nothing you cannot do. Others might be able to do it better but there is nothing you cannot do".

Under Miss MacQueen's guidance, the Camp Site at Castle Ashby was opened in 1935 and a lasting memory perpetrated as a result of the bequest after her demise, of her last home at Little House, in the village of Twywell. This excellent base for Guides provides facilities for recreation as well as overnight accommodation.

'BE PREPARED' – A PERSONAL RECOLLECTION

As a keen Girl Guide with a sleeve full of badges and leader of the Robin Patrol, I loved going to camp and was always eager to set up base in the grounds of Wadenhoe House, the home of Miss MacQueen, our County Commissioner.

It might have been during wartime, for petrol was rationed (by Ministry-issued coupons) and my father instructed me to stay put until collected at the appointed time, being about sixteen miles from Kettering, my home town.

The hammering of tent pegs with wooden mallets and for breakfast, huge 'doorsteps' of crusty bread, baked beans and bangers sizzling in a blackened pan over a camp fire. But first, snuggling down in a lumpy wadded bag beneath leaky canvas under a dark sky, where massive ancient trees cast mysterious shadows in the spooky night, was exciting!

Lost in the mist of time, I cannot recall my urgent reason to leave camp against my father's wishes, but I set off along the road to Aldwincle, bedroll on the back of my navy uniform. From my sturdy leather belt hung an enamel mug, my trusty multi-blade steel penknife

(with a gadget to remove stones from horse's hooves, though I never did!), plus a whistle.

I tramped along to the next village, Thorpe Waterville

Miss MacQueen – second officer from the left. Courtesy: The late Anne Beasley.

and slowly realised that it was, indeed, a long walk home! On reaching the main road at Thorpe Crossing, a country railway station, I started heading for the market town of Thrapston, now rather worried and caught between two distant towns. In my youth, young ladies did not hitchhike, so I sheepishly walked on the grass verge of the A605, head and thumb vaguely down.

A long, immaculate bonnet, preceded by a pair of enormous chrome headlights, slowly slid to a halt beside me and a cheery voice called:

"Hello, where are you off to?"

Hardly daring to glance up, I mumbled: "To Kettering".

"Jump in," said he, "I'm going your way."

Hesitantly, (although innocent and no thought of mugging or rape in those halcyon days) I stepped into the wide-open back door, glancing at the royal crest, to opulence! The upholstery was of blue velvet with plush carpets and dainty blinds with gold fringes, tassels and tiny vases, similar to ice cream cones, fixed to the window piers, holding little posies.

I sat, at first nervously, on the edge of the deep seat, as we glided along, slowing on the outskirts of Thrapston. Bystanders stopped to stare and gave me friendly waves and beaming smiles, the men even doffing their caps! Gaining confidence, I returned their greetings, as royalty were wont to do (this I had occasionally seen on Pathé Gazette News at the pictures) and by the time we reached Kettering, I was thrilled.

I asked the driver to drop me at the Corn Market Hall, at the top of my avenue, but he had plenty of time and insisted on knowing my house number, turning amid twitching lace curtains of these rather sedate residents.

I remember thinking that my father would be so proud of me, arriving in a royal limousine, but there he stood, very much the working man, thumbs in braces (with the style and figure of the cartoon character Andy Capp). He hurtled down the steps just as the uniformed chauffeur from Barnwell Castle, country seat of the Duke and Duchess of Gloucester, opened the rear door. Dad reached in, grabbed me by the collar and belt simultaneously and yanked me onto the pavement. He proceeded to toss me through the front door, loudly banishing me to my room. The driver stood open-mouthed and, no doubt, got an undeserved verbal lashing, poor man.

I was punished, not necessarily for accepting the ride, but for the act of disobedience – such was the mode of the day...
Mia

PRINCESS ALICE
DUCHESS OF GLOUCESTER
(1901–2004)

A genteel lady

L ADY ALICE CHRISTABEL DOUGLAS-SCOTT, third daughter of the 7th Duke of Buccleugh and his wife, was born on Christmas Day 1901, at Montagu House, Whitehall, London.

As one of eight children, educated by a string of governesses in her early years, she went on to boarding school at the age of 12, to West

Malvern, Worcestershire, and was enrolled at a finishing-school in Paris, before returning home two years later. She became a debutante, presented at Court and was invited to dance at Windsor Castle.

This was a period of country pursuits for the young woman and her peers, who enjoyed parties, racing at Ascot and tennis at Wimbledon, when her social circle included Prince Henry, third son of King George V and Queen Mary.

Lady Alice travelled the world at this time, to North and South

Courtesy: Northamptonshire Newspapers Ltd.

Africa and was taken to Boughton House, near Kettering, to convalesce after a serious bout of cerebral malaria. More journeys followed, before she became involved with the Girl Guide movement, Red Cross and the Voluntary Aid Detachment (V.A.D.).

Prince Henry proposed, was accepted, and the wedding was to take place at Westminster Abbey, but the demise of Alice's father, necessitated a change of plan and the ceremony proceeded in the chapel at Buckingham Palace in November 1935.

When King George V died, soon after the nuptials, Prince Henry became the Duke of Gloucester, when the couple had

Courtesy: Northamptonshire Newspapers Ltd.

to take up royal duties. Their first home was at the Royal Pavilion, Aldershot, and then a move to York House in London. In 1938 they purchased Barnwell Manor, a rambling Elizabethan residence with considerable farmland.

The popular royals were immediately in village life, particularly during World War II, when the Princess became head of the Women's Royal Air Force, with the rank of Air Chief Marshall, as well as the burgeoning 'Meals on Wheels' service and Presidency of the Royal College of Music.

A controversy arose in their public life when the couple were directed to visit the disgraced Duke and Duchess of Windsor, living in France, which caused much adverse comment, in 1938.

In 1945, the family, now including Princes William and Richard, born in 1941 and 1943 respectively, relocated to Australia, when their father was appointed the first Governor General, remaining there for two years, based in Canberra.

Returning to the United Kingdom in 1948, they took up a number of tours and commitments, continuing to add land to their Barnwell estate.

Sadly, at only 30 years old, Prince William perished in an air crash

in Staffordshire in 1972 and the Duke succumbed too, as a result of being incapacitated in a car accident several years earlier, in which his wife had been injured.

Prince Richard, succeeding to the title, married his Danish bride, Brigette Van Deurs, at Barnwell Church, who in turn, produced three grandchildren for Princess Alice.

The entire family moved to Kensington Palace in 1995, including the Princess and her precious dogs, Indie and Monty, leaving the manor and her beloved gardens, though her love for the countryside remained as she became increasingly frail. She finally retired in 2000 and the following year, celebrated her 100th birthday with members of the royal family, including her original bridesmaids, the Queen and Princess Margaret at the Palace. A military parade was held in her honour, when her favourite Scottish pipe bands took a leading role.

Princess Alice passed away in October 2004 and is remembered with affection, as a genteel lady, who never sought the limelight and loved by all who came close to her.

CAMEOS

ALICE OLD (Dates unknown)
A lady of longevity

ALICE OLD OF WEEDON, lived through the reigns of six monarchs and her grave in the churchyard records the story of her longevity.

Born in the time of Elizabeth I (1558–1603) on the Roman Watling Street at Weedon, she might have known of Drake and Raleigh and their explorations and of the infamous Gunpowder plot of 1605 in the reign of James I. Would she have known of the English Civil War of 1645 and the imprisonment of Charles I at Holdenby House, who had previously hunted at Fawsley Hall, the ancestral home of the Knightley family, prior to the Battle of Naseby? She could have witnessed armies from both sides and maybe the stragglers making their way back to their units after the Naseby conflict.

Then there were also the outbreaks of the Plague, the Great Fire of London and, much nearer to home, the Great Fire of Northampton in 1675.

History might have passed Alice by, for there was scant form of communication in those days, when most peasants could neither read nor write, or not immediately concerned with such affairs around them.

Alice died in the reign of William III and Mary II (1689–1702).

BOUDICCA (Died AD 62)
Legendary warrior queen

DR EDWARD SCOTT, acknowledged antiquarian on such matters, states that Boudicca, or more commonly Boadicea, was queen of the British people, widowed on the demise of her husband Prasutagus in AD 60.

Queen Boudicca. Courtesy: Colin Eaton.

The rulers of the Iceni tribe, actually in Norfolk, were fiercely opposed to the invasion of the cruel Roman forces, who abused Boudicca and her two daughters.

In hatred and revenge, the queen mobilised an army of barbarian rebels and plundered Roman holdings at Colchester, St Albans and London, but was defeated in an ensuing battle.

Failure in conquest was hard to bear and Boudicca took poison in an undisclosed location in AD 62. It is rumoured that her wealth of treasure was buried alongside her and is possibly located in Northamptonshire.

A document at of the time of Edward I (1272–1307) refers to land at Whittlebury and called 'Dead Queen Moor'.

Her vibrant image has been captured and cast in bronze, in an intimidating pose as a might warrior, upstanding in a terrifying chariot drawn by a pair of rearing horses. The plinth bears the date AD 61 and occupies a prestigious site on the corner of The Embankment, at the foot of Westminster Bridge in London.

CELIA FIENNES (1662–*c*.1712)
An extensive journey

AN INTREPID AND PERCEPTIVE TRAVELLER of distinction to pass through Northamptonshire in the 17th century was Celia Fiennes, born 1662 at Newton Toney, near Salisbury in Wiltshire, to prominent parents.

As a young woman, her epic journeys began to "regain my health" and proceeded to embrace every county in England, also crossing the border into Scotland, in a series of excursions on horseback.

She rode side-saddle, in all weathers, accompanied only by a servant to attend her needs, seeking food and lodging at inns, taverns, humble cottages, remote farms, or at the invitation of the local Squire at the manor in a grand house.

Celia must have encountered and endured endless discomforts and privations, owing to the poor state of the roads and the very real threat of highwaymen, who were rife at the time.

This incredible woman compiled not only a comprehensive survey of our English counties, but also detailed descriptions of all she observed, from cheese to linen, lace to teapots, fields to forests and rivers, industry, towns and cathedrals.

In passing, around 1712, her journal refers to Holdenby, an Elizabethan house "with towers almost like a Castle old built", and belonging to the "Earle of Fevershams". Althorp, splendid home of Charles Spencer, 3rd Earl of Sunderland, is described "lay low within a thicket of wood on all sides but the front where it appear'd like a Princes Court of brick and stone very fine".

Quotes from *The Illustrated Journeys of Celia Fiennes* (1682–*c*.1712), ed. Christopher Morris.

CHERRYNOSE (Dates unknown)
Conspicuous vagrant

CHERRYNOSE was a female character of undetermined age whose bulbous red nose shone like a beacon, who today might have been known as a 'bag lady'. She pushed a shabby old-fashioned perambulator around the streets of Kettering in the 1940s and was distinctive in a different way!

A scruffy felt hat was perched precariously on her matted locks and her garb always seemed to be of voluminous layers, wrinkled stockings falling about the ankles and down-at-heel shoes, perhaps missing a shoelace.

She took to any convenient doorway to sleep or the refuge of the Salvation Army and was often given food and accepted as a local tramp, of which there were many in the town. The steps of the public library were perhaps comfortable for her bulky form, where passing children would be wary of her presence.

Before the advent of the ubiquitous plastic bag, there were stout brown paper bags with string handles suffice to store goods such as rags and donated clothes. Wet things were wrapped in newspaper, especially greasy fish and chips, and an assortment of fizz and dark bottles jiggling together heralded her approach!

LADY HATTON (Dates unknown)
The guilt of a mother

A LETTER to Lord Hatton 1678. From the Finch-Hatton Collection at Northamptonshire Record Office.

> *"My deare Lord your last letter has giving me the greatest satisfaction in the world to hear that you have your health so well and that you take it so patently that you had not a boy. I am sore I did not, if the lose of my life would have procured you one. I hope you will have another wife that will be able to bring you one for I had rather be dead than alive, I am extreamely discontented more than ever I was for god knows when I shall get to you".* 16 Jan 1678.

GHOSTS GALORE

SURELY, no local book would be considered complete without a smattering of ghostly tales! There is a plethora of intriguing myths and legends, and almost every village and hamlet boasts of at least one!

THE MISTLETOE BOUGH
A legend of intrigue persists from Titchmarsh, close to Thrapston, where the castle site abuts the main street, opposite a pub.

In medieval times, William de Sidenham built a fine castle, which, in due course, passed to his daughter Maud, a ward of Henry III. This young woman married a wealthy titled gentleman, Sir John Lovell, in a lavish ceremony one Christmas Eve.

It was a grand occasion with much merriment in the great hall, with dancing to a troupe of musicians up in the gallery. The lofty walls were bedecked with greenery and mistletoe appropriate to the occasion and the festivities went on into the night.

The excited bride called for a game of hide and seek, dashing off to a hiding place she had discovered in childhood. Flying up the stone spiral staircase to her little secret chamber, she hurriedly climbed into a huge oak chest and the heavy lid banged down as she nestled on the fur rug lining the base, but she was trapped!

On being unable to find his wife, Sir John became sick with despair and, along with their guests, searched the castle for days, but no trace was found. Had she been kidnapped?

Years later, a female servant discovered the forgotten closet and the abandoned chest. After a tussle to open the hefty lid, a fright was caused by the macabre discovery of a fragile skeleton, draped with tatters of a silken gown and a jewelled circlet on the crumbling skull.

The Lovell family were in residence for 100 years, until they moved away from the county in the 14th century.

NANCY WEBB

The pathetic ghost of Nancy Webb is said to glide over the meadows at Passenham, a hamlet on the southern tip of the county.

The Crimean War was the setting for this tragic tale, when Nancy went to neighbouring Deanshanger for the annual feast. The pretty fair lass met a soldier at the jolly gathering and eventually they wed in the church at Passenham.

Nancy soon became pregnant and the pair were delighted at the birth of their first baby, though sadly, the father perished in battle. Already grief stricken, Nancy then suffered another blow when her dear infant died.

Prostrate with grief, her mind damaged, on the anniversary of their encounter, Nancy was seen, as if demented, to hurl herself into the mill stream, a tributary of the River Ouse and was instantly crushed by the massive mill wheel as it relentlessly revolved.

When the feast returns each October, Nancy's ghost is said to drift from the churchyard to the watermill. The sound of a splash follows, an eerie groan – then silence!

HANNAH SPARKE (1678–1785)
Woman of ingenuity

THE REGISTER of All Hallows' Parish Church in Wellingborough, which stands above the Market Place at the top of Pebble Lane, has the following entry and relates to a local woman, Hannah Sparke, the heroine of the day:

> *"On July 28 1738 happened a terrible fire at 2 of ye clock in the afternoon and in less than 4 hours consumed the best part of the town, it was a fryday".*

The fire broke out after an oat-drying kiln caught light and quickly spread, eventually destroying 205 houses in the town, where intense heat melted lead on the church roof. In the absence of water, Hannah gave the order that 'malt liquors' should be brought up from her cellars to quench the flames. Blankets soaked in beer were spread upon the thatched roof of her house in Pebble Lane.

Hannah's body, when she died at the age of 107 on 11 Sept 1785, was enclosed in a lead coffin, on whose lid was a crown and details of her life, in raised letters, placed below a slab in the north aisle. A tablet of white marble on the wall nearby is a tribute to her bravery in saving the town.

A tile imprinted with the date of the blaze on the back wall of business premises in Silver Street goes mostly unnoticed.

LADY ELEANOR FUCHS (1916–2003)
A perspicacious partner

LADY ELEANOR, late of Loddington, was the wife of Sir Vivian Fuchs, knighted for his achievement in heading the first trek across Antarctica in 1958, which was successfully accomplished in 99 days, who died in 1999. One of the mountains in the Shackleton Range was designated Honnywill Peak, to honour Lady Eleanor, taking the name from her first marriage.

Lady Eleanor ran the U.K. operation from the expedition's London base and wrote the account of the exploration *The Challenge of Antarctica* of the 2000 mile haul and the story of previous attempts, intended for use in schools and to inspire young people, which was published in 1969.

She died in April 2003 at Nazareth House in Northampton.

MARGARET KEEP (1853–1935)
Unrequited love?

MARGARET KEEP, born 1853, the eldest of five children, lived with the family at Keep House in Wollaston. Her siblings, a sister and three boys occupied the spacious dwelling with their parents, being built by Ambrose Dickens, lord of the manor in the 18th century.

Meticulous housekeeping accounts, as an adult, record the lifestyle of the period when the two girls were educated at home. Sister Alice ran a private school, teaching classic and artistic subjects, in addition to a well-attended Bible class in the village.

Apart from leading a typically quiet country life, Margaret sometimes visited relatives in Kensington and it was at this time and place that she became acquainted with Robert Browning, who was very much her senior, and his spinster sister Sarianna and often heard of the widower's son Pen, a painter of note residing in Venice.

Margaret revealed the joyous spate of Robert's intimate letters, to her mother, which sadly came to an abrupt end upon the demise of her elderly admirer in 1889. Was she, seemingly decorously wooed by the poet's wondrous way with words, in this era of genteel Victorian sensibilities?

The young woman was evidently impressed by the gracious hostess Sarianna, quoting exotic courses from delicious menus which she had shared with the family at their home in Warwick Crescent, Kensington.

Browning quoted his poems to Margaret, to which she was highly responsive to his words though, no doubt, a sense of decorum prevailed. She tells of visits to popular concerts and the thrill of being privy to such treasures as Tennyson's writings and a gift from another friend of that period, Rosetti. There were references too, to Browning's own forthcoming publications, sharing readings of his new works.

Those missives tell of her growing affection for the poet, although initially the relationship appeared platonic. The few telling pages hinted at the burgeoning

Courtesy: Loaned by Barry Robinson.

feelings for Robert Browning and contained descriptions of his London home bedecked with elegant furnishings conveyed from their villa in Florence, also mention of their new home in London.

The poet travelled often, leaving a void in the life of his young admirer and she treasured a present of a lace-edged handkerchief from St Moritz, given in 1887, as well as a Venetian brooch and a jet locket which she frequently favoured to wear. An Oriental-style bronze oil lamp was sent to Margaret after his death by Robert's daughter-in-law, when Sarianna became less hospitable.

Robert died in Italy in November 1889, sadly leaving Margaret to linger on bereft and alone, nursing her vivid memories of days gone by and her diary of a semblance of romance, for which she obviously yearned.

LADY VAUX (Dates unknown)
A plucky widow

FOR TWO CENTURIES the Vaux family lived at Harrowdon Hall and in the 16th century, the house became the refuge of Catholic priests.

Baron Vaux died in 1585, leaving his widow Elizabeth, a staunch supporter of the Catholic cause, with six children.

Lady Vaux was keen to set up a priest college and gave refuge to Jesuit John Gerard, hiding him in another of their properties at Irthlingborough. The authorities heard of this and searched the house but found nothing. Elizabeth had secured Kirby Hall with the intention of constructing a 'priest hole' and to this end, acquired the services of a carpenter, known to build such hiding places. This plan failed too and Lady Vaux then chose to favour Harrowden Hall for the purpose. Father Gerard moved in with the family and a wing was built for the priests next to the old chapel, with a secret chamber to conceal the holy men and a meeting place for members of the faith.

At the time of the Gunpowder Plot in 1605, Elizabeth came under suspicion again and a number of soldiers were dispatched to scour Harrowden Hall for a second time. Lady Vaux and her son, aged 17 years at the time, kept calm and appeared co-operative as the men ransacked each room for any trace of hidden fugitives.

Their trusted carpenter, Nicholas Owen, had constructed many such bolt-holes in the county and had created a clever ruse 'a hole within a hole'. Elizabeth was able to protect Gerard and managed to supply vital food and water undetected.

However, the search party came very close to the fugitive priest, but failed to discover the hole within!

Lord Salisbury, upon whose instruction the soldiers had been sent to search the Hall, issued an arrest warrant for Lady Vaux and that winter, she and her son were escorted to London, but never brought to trial, eventually returning to Harrowden Hall.

Father Gerard escaped the country and Nicholas Owen, the carpenter, was captured, tortured and was to die in prison.

The present imposing Hall was built around 1719, after the original house became dilapidated and untenable.

MARY, QUEEN OF SCOTS (1542–1587)
A tragic queen

NEARLY EVERYONE MUST KNOW of the poignant figure from history, Mary, Queen of Scots, but how many know that our county has the dubious honour of hosting her execution?

Mary had been imprisoned in the bleak Fotheringhay Castle which was situated on a large mound overlooking the water-meadows lining the River Nene. Only a fragment of the former castle and the rough mound now testifies to this turbulent period. In summer a mass of Scots thistles are scattered on the stony hill, and are known as Queen Mary's tears, aids this sombre setting.

On the 8 February 1587 she was led from her apartments in the castle to the banqueting hall and there beheaded. Afterwards her heart was buried in the grounds and her body embalmed and wrapped in a sheet and laid in a leaden coffin.

After a few months it was moved to Peterborough Cathedral where it was buried in a service conducted at night and attended by many of the county's aristocracy.

Twenty-five years later, on the orders of Mary's son James I, her coffin was exhumed and carried to London where it was interred in Westminster Abbey on 11 October 1612.

Courtesy: Northamptonshire Libraries and Information Services.

MRS GRAHAM (Dates unknown)
An intrepid flyer

A REPORT FROM Dakard's Stamford News of 1828, tells of "an adventurer" Mrs Graham of Northampton, who attempted an ascent in a balloon "which had been expanded for the purpose of taking up to 2 persons".

In moving it from the gas works, where it had been inflated, to the Market Square, a huge rip in the fabric causing escape of the gas, had resulted in a collision with some chimneys. The balloon was damaged to such an extent, that it was thought prudent to carry only one person, hence the intrepid Mrs Graham.

The "vessel", already previously damaged by a slash of almost one foot, had to be abandoned by the fearless lady, who had to jump out of the balloon and into "Widow Ager's attic window" to safety when the balloon collided with another chimney!

Apparently, it floated up and away, to eventually come to ground at Tansor, near Oundle. The basket fell into the River Nene, where the villagers were concerned by the absence of the navigator, until it was explained by a person who had followed the lone flight!

QUEEN HENRIETTA (1609–1669)
A royal dip?

QUEEN HENRIETTA, wife of Charles I, journeyed to Wellingborough in 1628, with her husband and royal entourage, to partake of the chalybeate waters, for which the small town was becoming well-known.

The party stayed at The White Swan and visited The Red Well, located at the eastern end of Kilborn Road.

The wells are depicted on Wellingborough's coat of arms, as a reminder of what might have been – famous for its health-giving waters and recognition as a spa town!

ST WERBURGH (Died *c.*705)
Geese begone!

IN THE FAR-OFF DAYS of Mercian rule, King Ethelred appointed his niece, St Werburgh to administer the priory at Weedon.

Courtesy: Church of St Peter and St Paul, Weedon Bec.

The local villagers had been greatly distressed by a flock of geese that had descended on the fields, decimating their precious crops. The despairing folk turned to St Werburgh in their hour of need, to drive away the ravaging birds. It was said that she responded to their plea by the power of prayer and the geese were banished from the parish, never to return to Weedon.

The church of St Peter, with its Norman tower and 19th century chancel and nave, nestles beneath the embankment of the Grand Union Canal and the railway line and high viaduct, has a weathervane depicting a goose and, in the stained glass, a memorial to the saint.

St Werburgh is buried in Chester Cathedral.

WITCHES
Wicked women

WITCHCRAFT, in this country, was considered to be at its peak in the 17th and early 18th century, when wicked witches were rife, particularly in the more isolated countryside communities.

Such people were frequently held responsible for many traumas and tragedies, both those inflicted on human beings as well as animals. Not only did they concoct and dispense potions, but cast spells that terrified their victims, and some were held accountable for all manner of deeds and misfortunes.

A woodcut of three women riding on a sow is thought to be the title page of a lengthy pamphlet telling of mischief, and reads thus: "before the apprehension, this Agnes Browne, one Katherine Gardiner and Joan

Three witches "riding on a sowe's back".

Lucas, all birds of a winge and all abiding in the Towne of Guilsborough did ride one night to a place (not above a mile off) Ravensthorp, all upon a sowe's back".

Described in the pamphlet are Agnes Browne and her daughter Joan Vaughan, well-known for their churlish behaviour, and shunned by their neighbours at Guilsborough. The younger woman, Joan, verbally attacked a gentlewoman, Mistress Belcher, who became visibly distressed and fled to her home in fear.

The two evil women plotted against the victim and cast a spell upon her, causing agonizing pain and confusion. Her brother tried to approach the cursers and came to the conclusion that the Devil was responsible for his own inability to retaliate, as he felt physically restrained by an unseen force when he tried to confront the pair, where the Devil was guarding the door.

He eventually called the authorities and the two were arrested, cautioned and then sent home. The injured parties tried to obtain further evidence of witchcraft, but did not succeed. On their return journey home, the coach was accosted by a pair of riders on horseback, who threatened them with death. Frightened and fearful for their safety, it transpired that one of the horses dropped down dead, but not the humans!

Another case is recorded of Helen Jenkenson of Thrapston, known to bewitch cattle. Mistress Mulso, who had made an accusation against her causing the death of a child, insisted that the woman be examined for certain 'witch marks', when evidence of an intimate nature, which was suspected, was indeed, discovered.

The following day, the accuser's washing hanging out to dry, had been daubed with obscenities and she immediately challenged the witch to restore the clothes to cleanliness, which was done. The perpetrator was taken to court, but they failed to force a confession.

Elinor Shaw of Cotterstock and Mary Phillips of Oundle, were said to 'have pawned their soules to the Devil in exchange for evil powers' with which they levelled both on folk and cattle.

On Wednesday 7 March 1705, they were brought to the Assizes at

Northampton and arraingned for 'Bewitching and Tormenting in a Diabolical manner' a woman, Mrs Robert Wise of Benefield and a child of four years, and also 'Bewitching to Death' twelve-year-old Charles Ireland of Southwick.

Both women pleaded not guilty at the same time, when animal deaths were also quoted. Both eventually confessed to the crimes in a lengthy and gruesome statement, giving intimate details of the lurid dealings with the Devil. Found guilty on all charges amid a considerable amount of pandemonium in court, the death penalty was imposed 'To be Hang'd till they are almost Dead, and then surrounded with Faggots, Pitch and other Combustible matter, which being Set on Fire, their Bodies are to be consumed to Ashes. 8th March 1705'. This was purported to be the last ever execution of witches in this county.

The repeal of the Witchcraft Act came into being in 1736, bringing to a close this period of accusation and punishment.

There are differing accounts of witches' trials and of the imposed executions and other cases have unconfirmed conclusions.

Death penalties for witches in Salem, Massachusetts, U.S.A. also involved an horrific end for the convicted, when each victim was securely bound between two boards or planks, laid on the floor and trod upon until the victims were pulverized to death.

ABOUT THE AUTHORS

Mia Butler divides her so-called 'leisure time' between writing books (11 in total) on country walking in her native county, as well as more 'off'beat' subjects such as *Learn Yersalf Northamptonshire Dialect*.

Her lifetime interest has been in travel and the marine environment, and she has worked in a facet of conservation, specifically whales of the Pacific Ocean.

Born on the Racecourse at Northampton, Mia definitely qualifies as a writer of local status.

Colin Eaton is a Northampton man – born and bred in the town where he still lives, working in local government and, during the 1980s, being extensively involved in the Oral History Project organised by the Leisure and Libraries department of the Northamptonshire County Council.

Colin has been interested in county history for many years, being awarded the University of Leicester Certificate in Local History.

ACKNOWLEDGEMENTS

Our sincere thanks are extended to all our friends and colleagues who kindly contributed facts and photographs toward the collection of this montage of fascinating females.

We hope we have left no-one out, but apologise if our negligence has caused displeasure!

Hilary Bailey, the late Anne Beasley, David Blagrove, Judy Bradley, Bernie Burgess, Sue Burt, Nicholas Butler, Sheila Carr, Chris Covington, Richard Field, Mr & Mrs Napier, Marian Pipe, Sally Randall, The Reverend Helen Rayment, Barry Robinson, Mary Robinson, Julian Royle, Nancy Seymour, Rashmi Shah, John & Margo Simpson, Mavis Thornton, Clare Trend, Cordelia Troop, Ian and Sally Ward, Nancy Weare USA, British Waterways, Northamptonshire Libraries and Information Service, and Northampton Newspapers Ltd.

BY THE SAME AUTHORS

LEARN YERSALF
NORTHAMPTONSHIRE DIALECT

A compilation of anecdotes, familiar phrases and words
from a bygone era, all now fast disappearing – some,
these days, are even labelled 'politically incorrect. Ask the
average Northamptonshire person about the county accent
or dialect and they will probably be unaware there is such a
thing – *that* is why 'this here' book was compiled!

Priced at £5.99

Local titles published
by John Nickalls Publications

**A GARLAND
OF WAVENEY VALLEY TALES**
A compilation of illustrated tales from
Suffolk of yesteryear.

A LEVEL COUNTRY
Sketches of its Fenland folk and history.

A PHARMACIST'S TALE
The joys, delights and disappointments
encountered preserving pharmacy
history.

CURIOSITIES OF NORFOLK
A county guide to the unusual.

CURIOSITIES OF SUFFOLK
A county guide to the unusual.

GREAT OUSE COUNTRY
Sketches of its riverside folk and history
from source to mouth.

**MELTON CONSTABLE, BRISTON
& DISTRICT – BOOK ONE**
A portrait in old picture postcards.

**MELTON CONSTABLE, BRISTON
& DISTRICT – BOOK TWO**
A further portrait in old picture
postcards.

**NATURE TRAILS IN
NORTHAMPTONSHIRE**
A series of illustrated walks.

NEWMARKET, TOWN AND TURF
A pictorial tour.

NORTH NORFOLK
A portrait in old picture postcards.

NORWICH – THEN AND NOW
A look at the city through old postcards
and modern photographs.

**IN AND AROUND NORWICH –
THEN AND NOW**
A further look at Norwich and district.

**HARWICH, DOVERCOURT
AND PARKESTON – VOL 3**
A further selection of old picture
postcards.

NORWICH – THEN AND NOW
A third selection of old picture postcards.

**ROBBER BARONS AND
FIGHTING BISHOPS**
The Norman influence in East Anglia.

SHIRES, SALES AND PIGS
The story of an Ely family of
Auctioneers. George Comins,
1856–1997.

SUFFOLK'S LIFEBOATS
A portrait in postcards and photographs.

S'WONDERFUL
A symphony of musical memories.

'SMARVELLOUS
More musical memories.

**TIPPLE & TEASHOP RAMBLES
IN NORTHAMPTONSHIRE**
A series of illustrated walks.

**WALKS IN THE WILDS OF
CAMBRIDGESHIRE**
A series of illustrated walks.

WICKEN: A FEN VILLAGE
A third selection of old pictures.